RE-BUILDING THE FRONT PORCH OF AMERICA

Other Books by Patrick Overton

The Leaning Tree, collected poetry

Grassroots & Mountain Wings
the arts in rural and small communities (editor)

Spanning Cultures Through Arts Education (editor)

RE-BUILDING THE FRONT PORCH OF AMERICA

ESSAYS ON THE ART OF COMMUNITY MAKING

PATRICK OVERTON

Published in 2001 in the United States of America by
    PrairieSea Press
    964 17th Street
    Astoria, Oregon 97103
    503 338-6218

ISBN 0-9708229-0-1
Library of Congress Control Number: 2001130086

Cover design by C. Patrick Hanna

Printed and bound in the United States of America

FIRST EDITION - Second Printing

This book is dedicated to Boonville, Missouri, where I first learned the craft and the potential of community arts development; and to Dr. Lee Cary, mentor, colleague, and friend, who guided me in the discovery of how this potential can be fulfilled by rebuilding the front porch of America.

Table of Contents

Foreword

I first met Patrick Overton at Eau Claire, Wisconsin, where he delivered the major address for a statewide arts conference. His keynote was entitled "Rebuilding the Front Porch of America." It connected with full intensity and appreciation with his audience. Part of Patrick's appeal is that he cares about his public speaking as meticulously as he does his writing. Part of his appeal is that what he says reflects an analysis, and offers a prescription for problems in our society which are steeped in the "common sense" he envisions for America.

In hearing and reading Patrick Overton, one's reactions alternate between "Eureka! A fresh insight!" or "This guy just put into words what I've been brooding about!" This book, combining philosophy and praxis in the context of the cultural battles in our nation, creates such reactions. We will be better in our community life for reading it and for taking Patrick Overton to heart.

As the Mayor of Amery, Wisconsin, a former state legislator chairing the Arts Committee, a United Methodist minister, promoter of the arts, and a longtime reader and admirer of Robert Gard, I do take Patrick to heart. He does speak profoundly to the future of my community.

Our "City of Lakes," Amery, is nearing 3,000 residents and is on the outer ring of "Penturbia," the fifth circle of growth surrounding the St. Paul-Minneapolis metropolitan area. Already, villages along the St. Croix River border are beginning to look like extensions of suburban shopping strips. Our community is nearing high noon to maintain its own unique identity, control growth, and to preserve Mrs. Johnson's trees in lieu of another fast food joint.

Our community was recently listed in the *100 Best Small Art Towns in America* by John Vallani. A month ago, the Northern Lakes Center for the Arts and its founders, LaMoine and Mary Ellen MacLaughlin, were given Wisconsin's highest award for the arts by our Governor at his home. A few weeks earlier Amery's community education program, a Chautauqua smorgasbord of arts and education offerings, was given a state award for educational excellence. Our city library has the highest per capita usage in Wisconsin, and provides a staff person to lead book discussions in senior citizen apartment buildings. We are integrating grade school and high school youth into city commissions. We are proud to discuss openly the role of the arts in community-making. Our cultural and spiritual identity is not lost in the traditional debates over potholes and the politics surrounding planning and zoning.

Amery, I believe, is not unique in its acceptance of the arts as a catalyst for community-making. Patrick Overton tells the truth about rural genius. There truly exists in many small towns in America, a willingness to explore new ideas, and a mother lode of talent.

Last week, I had a chance discussion over coffee with a fly-tying expert and a high school educated farmer about a book we had all read, *New York Days*, Willie Morris' reminiscences of his tenure as editor of *HARPER'S* and the political and cultural turmoil of the 1960's. Last summer, a Northern Lakes community theatre group revised Ibsen's, *An Enemy of the People*, into a contemporary local setting, never losing an ounce of power from Ibsen's message. Northern Lakes also exhibited the paintings of Jens Rasmussen, a local "Grandpa Moses". The arts are not captive to the Guthrie theatre, Walker Art Center, nor to an *Utne Reader* salon. The cafes and bakeries on the main streets of America, lousy coffee and all, and our small town art centers serve up some genius, too.

Patrick Overton recognizes that our communities are filled with storytellers and good stories. I like his work best when Patrick tells stories about the life-changing, community-making process of art. The stories of Greg, the Conrad Birdie of Boonville, and the Memorial Day event in Huntsville have the spirit of Frederick Buechner or Wendell Berry in their telling. I admire Patrick's ability to capture the wise phrase (the "Uncivil War"), create a revealing metaphor ("art is the unconditional grace of the imagination"), or share an insightful image (the replacement of the public front porch by the private back deck).

Patrick also is not afraid to engage in controversy. The segment in this book from his testimony before Congress on the National Endowment for the Arts should be widely disseminated.

At the same time, he is provocative on the direction of the leadership of the arts in the nation. Unlike many, he recognizes the pitfalls of utter dependence on public funding. He argues the need for the arts community to listen to the religious and cultural right, for, as he says, "They are our audience."

As one who has navigated the turbulent waters of the arts and political life for the past decade, I know that it is good to have Patrick Overton's voice and experience cutting away the rhetorical underbrush of extremism, and calling us each step of the way to the common ground and the positive shared values of community. The small steps of reconciliation are being taken around us in small ways every day. In one town nearby, fundamentalists and theological liberals are meeting for breakfast and a discussion of each previous night's installment of Bill Moyers' PBS series on Genesis. In another place, public school teachers, students, and community leaders are meeting to enact the multi-cultural, multi-generational integration sought by Patrick Overton.

I look forward to the day when Bill Moyers will interview Patrick Overton on PBS, and when this book will be the text of choice for arts boards and agencies, and college classrooms in America.

Finally, I am appreciative of the words of counsel Patrick offers to community arts agency administrators and workers. The advice for avoiding burnout, replicating successes, and serving as a navigator rather than as a one-person show, will be welcomed in local community arts programs. I once had a poster of Mark Twain in my office, with his observation that, "I have known a great many troubles in my lifetime -- most of which never happened." The front porch, after all, is a place for relaxed conversation and creative vision.

As I finish writing these comments, I am at the kitchen table looking directly out onto an old-fashioned front porch. Now, in winter, the porch floor is covered with bird seed and sunflower seeds. Nine different species are feeding, ranging from chickadees to cardinals. Despite the presence of uncivil crows and blue jays perched midway on the snowy lawn, they feast. I think they may be planning a show.

When the snow is gone and the show is over, the porch rocker species will go out to drink iced tea or sip some lemonade. They will talk about values, the direction of the country, and what they lately have seen or read. They will tell stories. They may even plan a show. Patrick Overton may not be in the conversation, but he will be present in spirit, rebuilding our front porch with style and substance.

HARVEY STOWER, Mayor
Amery, Wisconsin

Preface

This book is about two subjects: Community and the role of the arts in community-making. I have written it because I believe we are increasingly losing our "sense of community" and this threatens the future of our society. I also wrote it because I believe the arts contribute to community-making by rebuilding the front porch of America.

When I talk about community in this book, I talk primarily about rural and small communities. Almost all of my experience in community-making is in the rural and small community context and this is what I feel most qualified to discuss. But I do not use the term rural and small community to limit its application. In fact, it is intended to be broadly interpreted. As I say in the book, community is more a "state of mind" than it is a "place of residence." Community isn't defined by where we live as much as it is by the relationships we have with the people where we live. What I do know is that when a community gets too large, it is difficult to keep the sense of community that started it. But I know there are many large population centers where community arts development work is successful because it focuses on the people who live there and what they share together. The material in this book is applicable in any setting. I have spent the past ten years translating the material into the context of higher education, focusing on the role of the arts in campus community development.

I had multiple audiences in mind in writing this book. First and foremost, I was thinking of those people engaged directly in community-making through the community arts development process. This includes the paid and non-paid staff (community arts administrators) who work with and in the rural and small community setting. This also includes the countless volunteers, boards of directors and executive committees who keep community arts alive and vibrant. Second, it is written for people who are involved in various aspects of community-making, but have yet to discover the unique contribution the arts make to this process in rural and small communities. Third, it is written for people who are concerned about the changing nature of community in our society and want to find ways to rebuild the front porch of America.

This book is about community-making through the community arts development process. To do this, I look at who we are, what we do, how we do it, and why we do it.

The first section in the book provides a picture of the inscape of rural and small communities. By inscape, I mean the way community works - from the inside - people and the way they communicate with each other, the way they relate to each other; the shared values, interests, and concerns that bond them together. This is where I discuss who we are as community makers and what it is we do in the community arts development process.

The second section is practice-oriented, focusing on the individuals and organizations involved in the community arts development process. It is here I attempt to define, describe, and explain the role the arts play in community-making. This is where I discuss how we go about doing our community arts development work, including the challenges and opportunities facing those of us who have chosen community-making as our life's work.

The third section is about values. As a result, it is more personal and philosophically oriented than the first two sections. It is here I share my understanding of the meaning of art and the essential role it plays in the development of the human community. This is where I discuss why it is we do what we do as community makers. The book is written to encourage discussion among people of differing views and perspectives, much like the early historical tradition of people gathered together on their front porches and in their parlors. It is written to encourage people to identify and communicate more effectively about the important role of community arts development in the community-making process. It is my hope it will serve as a catalyst for many conversations about the important role the arts play in our lives and in our communities.

Acknowledgments

I had two choices when I wrote this book. The first was to cite every author and practitioner who has influenced me, which would be an almost insurmountable task. The second was to include a comprehensive resource bibliography in the back of the book. I have chosen the latter, including a selection of books relating to the community arts development movement and to organizational communications theory. In particular, I encourage the reading of all works by Alfred Arvold, Baker Brownell, Robert Gard, and Wendell Berry. Additional authors who have greatly influenced my work include psychologist M. Scott Peck, communication philosopher Georges Gusdorf, and theologian Paul Tillich.

All but two of the essays in this book are based on previously published articles, speeches, and workshops while I was Director of the Columbia College Center for Community & Cultural Studies (1987-1995). While these original presentations have been greatly revised and rewritten for this book, there are numerous individuals and organizations I need to acknowledge:

Rebuilding the Front Porch of America, is based on a speech I first delivered to the state meeting of the Wisconsin Assembly of Local Arts Councils in the fall of 1995. It was preparing for this speech that convinced me I needed to write this book. I also wish to acknowledge the National Assembly of Local Arts Agencies (now Americans for the Arts). They used the title to this book as the theme for their National Rurals Pre-Conference held before their national convention in St. Louis, 1996. I presented the keynote address for this pre-conference, expanding the presentation I made in Wisconsin. These two speeches greatly influenced this essay;

Nurturing the Invisible Culture of Rural Genius was originally part of a 1993 report submitted to the Southern Illinois Cultural Alliance (SICA) as part of a two-year, NEA funded community cultural planning process for the southern 34 counties of Illinois. In 1994, I expanded this theme for use as a keynote address that I delivered to the Community Arts Development conference held at the University of Saskatchewan in Saskatoon, Saskatchewan, Canada. I want to acknowledge Dr. Harold Baker and Kate Hobin, co-directors of this conference, and thank them for inviting me to contribute to and become part of the community arts development work in Canada;

Surviving the Values Collision is the result of an article commissioned by Romalyn Tilghman, editor of *Arts Rag* magazine. Close friend and colleague, Romalyn served as one of my pre-publication readers and I am grateful to her for her invaluable editing suggestions for this book;

Porches & Parlors is based on one of the chapters of my Ph.D. dissertation. It was later published in its first form by the National Assembly of Local Arts Agencies as part of *The Arts in Rural Areas Information Exchange.* It has appeared in various forms since then, including a chapter in the book, *Grassroots & Mountain Wings: the arts in rural and small communities,* published by the Columbia College Center for Community & Cultural Studies in 1992;

The Art of Community Making is based on an article published in the NALAA Quarterly Connections in 1987 entitled "Arts Development in Rural and Small Communities." This was my first published article in this field and was commissioned by Barbara Schaffer Bacon, editor of the magazine. The essay *Grassroots & Mountain Wings* was also first published in the NALAA Quarterly Connections in 1988;

Public Trust? was first presented as a paper at the Fourth National Conference on Ethics in America in 1993. This paper was published with an addendum later that same year as a part of the NALAA Monographs Series;

Navigating White Water in a Leaky Raft was first created as a workshop for the Southern Illinois Cultural Alliance. In addition, I also wish to acknowledge the Cedar City Arts Council, the Saskatchewan Assembly of Arts Councils; the British Columbia Assembly of Arts Councils, the Raintree Arts Council and the Huntsville Christian Church, for their contribution in working with me to develop the organizational design I discuss in this essay.

The Deep Voice and *Metaphor-The Final Freedom*, two new essays, represent the culmination of five years of work and research in conjunction with the Arts and Values Project at the Columbia College Center for Community & Cultural Studies. I wish to acknowledge the participants in this project who significantly influenced my thinking and writing on the relationship between arts and values. This group consists of Cindy Clair, Pat Courtney Gold, Davina Grace Hill, Sharon Morgan, David Nelson, Harriette Small, Romalyn Tilghman, Chris Van Antwerp, and Naj Wikoff.

Because this book represents a culmination of twenty years of work in the community arts development field, there are a number of additional acknowledgments I want to make. First, the Friends of Historic Boonville, my partners for 8 ½ years in creating the Boonville Community Arts Program.

Second, the Missouri Association of Community Arts Agencies. In particular, the Community Arts Administrators Network (MACAA/CAAN). These individuals consented to be part of my dissertation research project and became the group with whom I tested out my theories and models concerning training and professional and organizational development. They were patient and enthusiastic in support of my efforts. These are my colleagues and I owe them much.

Third, the members of the Asian Pacific Confederation for Arts Education. My experience as director of this international organization greatly broadened my understanding of the important role the arts, in particular, arts education can play in promoting cultural diversity and intercultural communication.

Fourth, the Turtle Creek Chorale, in particular, Dr. Tim Seelig, Artistic Director. This organization and the incredible people in it continue to teach me about the relationship between art and healing.

In addition, there are several close friends I want to thank: Naj Wikoff, who has been a continual source of support and encouragement; Maryo Ewell, who represents, in every way, the very best of what community arts development means; Ralph Burgard, who has been a great influence in my professional development, and Chris Van Antwerp, whose friendship and professional partnership has been a source of joy for the last fifteen years. I want to thank my colleagues at Columbia College who have contributed significantly to my work, especially Professor David O'Hagan, and my best friend, Professor Sidney Larson, who will never know how much he influenced the writing of this book. I also want to thank my students at the College. The essay, *Metaphor - The Final Freedom*, was written with them in mind. They are my teachers and I have learned much from them.

I want to thank my friends and colleagues most closely associated with this book - Mary Altman, Steve Duchrow, and LaMoine MacLaughlin. Serving as pre-publication readers, their insights and comments greatly influenced the final manuscript and I am deeply grateful for their contribution to this book. Were it not for LaMoine MacLaughlin's persistent encouragement, this book might not have been written. In addition, I wish to acknowledge Kevin Burchfield, my student assistant from 1995/96. And, last, but certainly not least, Jenny LaChance, my Administrative Assistant during the writing of this book. I cannot speak enough of her professionalism, commitment, and contribution to this publication. As a young person newly entering the field of community arts development, she speaks highly for the future of our profession.

Finally, I want to thank my wife, Lindi. She has been with me the entire adventure of the last twenty years. She has shared the joys, the disappointments, the struggles and the triumphs. She has always been a source of encouragement. She has always been there. She is my partner, in every way.

Introduction

We used to gather together on the front porch - families, friends, neighbors. Not for any special reason, just to be together, to converse with each other. That was enough. We had the time and we had the inclination. We would sit while refreshing summer breezes blew across the veranda - some sitting on a swing, some rocking back and forth in white wicker chairs, some leaning on the porch rail or on the steps. This is where we shared news about our lives, talked about the events going on around us, and caught up with each other as family, friends, neighbors and community. This was how we shared life and how we made meaning. This was also how we made community. It was intentional. It was spontaneous. It was fun.

We are losing our front porch. We are losing our gathering place. It is being replaced with decks in the back yard and contemporary architecture dominated by the garage, showcasing the treasured symbol of our mobility and freedom - the automobile. We move fast and we move in a lot of different directions. We learn a lot and we learn it quickly - but we don't always know what to do with what it is we learn.

Our culture is slowly "dis-integrating." We are losing our center and losing touch with the core values that keep us together as a community, perhaps even as a nation. We are untethered, disconnected from each other. Some feel isolated and alone. We are a society that is drifting and confused - unsure of the roles and the rules - caught in the middle of a social and economic upheaval. Everything around us is in transition and we just can't seem to keep up. And, while there are many exciting and positive things happening around us, even this is a source of stress because it brings about change and all change is stressful.

This is especially true in the thousands of rural and small communities all across our country. Traditionally resistant to change and insulated from outside cultural influences, America's rural and small communities have undergone enormous social and economic upheaval during the second half of this century. And there is no indication this is going to let up any time soon. This upheaval has presented many of our rural and small communities with challenges. The economic base has changed drastically. Young people continue to leave their communities and not return, draining essential human resources from already dwindling populations. And, even though there is an increasing number of people moving into these communities from metropolitan areas, many are bringing with them the very expectations and negative attitudes that caused them to want to leave in the first place. Life in rural and small community America just isn't what it used to be.

Where do the arts fit in this picture of communities in change and transition? Everywhere. Because of the work of community arts development, the arts have increasingly become part of the daily life of citizens who live in these communities. The arts invite us to tell our stories and listen to the stories of those around us. Community arts bring people of all ages, genders, races, religions, and economics together for the common good of sharing and celebrating who we are as individuals and as communities. This is what we are about when we do community arts development. We help people make art. And, in the process, we help people make community. Without really knowing it, community arts development has always been about the important work of rebuilding the front porch of America.

But, there is a problem. Hardly anyone has noticed what we have been doing. We never have been terribly successful at getting much public funding for the work we were doing with the arts in rural and small communities. Now, just at the time we should be able to make our case and take advantage of public support for our community arts development work, the public funding resource is dwindling. It may even disappear all together. And we have been so busy doing the work, we failed to do what is essential when pioneering new territory - we didn't create enough maps so others could follow. By the time we finally got around to making the maps, the social geography of the communities with which we were working had changed, and many of the maps were outdated before they could be used.

Unfortunately, over this past decade, this problem has been compounded by something none of us involved in the arts ever imagined - the arts have become the lightning rod for a lot of the "dis-comfort" and "dis-ease" people feel. Suddenly, those of us convinced we had found a way to rebuild the front porch of America and were busy going about that work, found ourselves accused of creating the very problem we thought we were solving. And while this problem has manifested itself primarily at the national level, those of us working in rural and small communities are increasingly finding ourselves caught in the crossfire of a growing political, cultural, and religious war. By the very nature of what the arts are (expression) and what they do (express the struggle of what it means to be human), the arts have become confused with the problems and the pain about which they so eloquently and authentically communicate. Many of us engaged in community arts development process find ourselves doing more community-sustaining than community-making. We spend more and more of our time and energy trying to keep in place what we thought we had already accomplished. The problem with this is that community is not static - it is always changing. There is no such thing as cultural status-quo. If it is not dynamic it is dying.

There are a lot of reasons why we should be discouraged. But, there are a lot more reasons why we shouldn't. That is what this book is about - not only why our community arts development work is important, but also why it is more essential now than ever before. And while it is not easy to work in a confused, changing, and sometimes uncomfortable environment, someone has to do it. Someone has to have the creative courage to see beyond the discomfort and envision the possibilities. Someone has to have the conviction to stand up in the midst of the social disintegration surrounding us and be about the business of community-making. Someone has to have the commitment to do the work of rebuilding the front porch of America. We are that someone.

But we cannot be about business as usual. If we are to take advantage of the opportunities facing us, we must be more determined and persistent now than ever before. What is required of us is creative and innovative thought. Our arts organizations and cultural institutions have to reinvent and redefine themselves.

We need to design and implement dynamic, flexible organizational systems that anticipate and thrive in change and transition. We need to identify the values driving our community arts development work, exploring the relationship between the arts and healing, spirituality, and diversity. And finally, it is essential that we create new strategies to help people understand the important role the arts play in our communities. If ever there was a time when we need to communicate more effectively who we are, what we do, and why we do it - it is now.

This book examines these issues. It is written to celebrate those who have dedicated their lives to community-making in rural and small communities. It is written to recognize and acknowledge their vital work in rebuilding the front porch of America. It is also written to celebrate the creative and cultural wealth that already exists within these communities and the incredible people with whom we work.

The front porch is a powerful metaphor to discuss how this nation can once again make community like we used to make community - by being together, by sharing, and most important of all, by communicating with each other, as human beings. Large or small, Victorian or Cape Cod, stoop or veranda, the front porch is symbolic of a place where we can meet and welcome the stranger and friend alike. Be it the concert hall, the arts center, the school auditorium, the town square or park, an old restored theater, church sanctuary, or in our homes - the new front porch must be a place where we can communicate unconditionally with each other. We must create places where we not only recognize and value diversity but also learn to accept the differences between us as the strength of our social fabric, not the cause of its frayed edges. Community arts development can do this. Community arts development can help us create a common ground where we can all be together. If we are successful, we can renew our sense of place, our sense of purpose, our sense of community. Perhaps, in the process, we can even rekindle the very "Common Sense" that brought this nation into existence. If we are successful, we will be doing the exciting and important work of rebuilding the front porch of America.

Part I
The Changing Inscape of Communities in America

Rebuilding the Front Porch of America

The first time I heard the word "home place," I was visiting one of my parishioners in the small, rural church I was serving in Arrow Rock, Missouri (population 81). Elizabeth, a young woman in her late twenties, and I were sitting on the swing at the home place where she grew up.

Discussing her impending role as a new mother she pointed to a room at the front of the house and said, "My grandmother was born in that room, my mother was born in that room, and I was born in that room. I want my child born in that room, too." These are roots. This defines what a home place is - not just years of history in one place, but generations of story, an emotional and spiritual tether connecting people with their past.

This is what we have lost; the physical and spiritual connection to our families and our community. We have lost that tether because we don't have very many home places any more and the ones we have are at risk - in disrepair, both physically and spiritually. Elizabeth was unable to give birth in that room because of complications. She and her family no longer live in that house, they built a new one. It doesn't have a front porch.

Last year I spoke at the statewide conference of community arts councils in Wisconsin. Their conference theme was "Bringing it All Back Home." I found the theme intriguing. As I reflected on bringing it all back home, I couldn't help but think of the home to which we are bringing it all back. I realized how dramatic the changes have been in our communities during this century, especially the second half. I also looked at what I have witnessed over the years of my work in the community arts field. The home-place is at risk - both physically and symbolically. There are many reasons for this: economic, political, and social. But it is an unshakable truth that many of our rural and small communities are in trouble. What is also true is that our "sense of community" is at risk as well.

Let's look at the metaphor of the front porch. It may be an idealized picture but it is a powerful image, nonetheless. The front porch was a place where people would gather and share. The front porch was where people would sit and talk with their families and friends. It was where people would visit their neighbors who were out for a walk. The front porch was a place where people could stay in touch with each other and what was happening around them. The front porch was an open invitation to gather together and share.

We don't build front porches any more. We build decks and put them in the backyard, sharing them only with those who we invite. This is how we protect ourselves. Now we are building "gated communities," a steady, slow return to the Mediaeval city-state, city-fortress concept where the stranger is viewed as an enemy to be kept out. And we build symbolic walls more powerful than those built of brick and stone. As a result, the social fabric of our communities becomes more frayed and tattered each day. We cater to the fear and discomfort people feel and we don't get to know people the way we used to know them. This phenomenon is occurring in our rural and small communities as well as our larger, metropolitan/suburban areas. No place is exempt.

The front porches of our society are creaky, leaky, and sagging. The roof is threatening to fall in, the swing dangles from one chain, precariously hanging on . . . refusing to give in to the creeping, destructive path of rust. . . the paint is peeling off the floor boards, and the rail is broken with pieces having disappeared years ago. Yet, it tenaciously refuses to surrender and be ignored. It hangs on in hope that someday, perhaps soon, we will return to it and realize it needs to be repaired. Some people renovating homes today are placing great value on restoring the front porch. It is an indication that people are looking for something to bring us together. For the most part, our community front porches - our social gathering opportunities - sit in disrepair as well. Unused and unrecognized for their important place in our lives. Many of them have simply ceased to exist. And we increasingly find ourselves not getting together any more, losing touch with each other. We are forgetting what it means to be a neighborhood, a community. Many of us live with a longing to return to the way community used to be, even if we don't know for sure what that really was. What we do know is our sense of community isn't what we want it to be.

The Death of Metaphor

Another problem we are facing in this country is the death of metaphor. We are watching the slow, steady decline of the imagination. This is especially true for many of our younger people. When I teach my classes at Columbia College, I always require a project of each student's own choosing in an attempt to encourage creativity. There is no grade; they get the points if they follow through on what they agreed to do. What they do isn't important as long as it applies to the class. I am always amazed at how resistant my students are to this invitation to be self-determined. They moan and groan about having to come up with something creative. Some of them resent the request. For some, it is actually torture.

A few years ago, a student in one of my communication classes struggled to choose a project. He had a wonderfully natural, deep-resonant voice, and I suggested he might want to consider a project that involved some work at our local community radio station. His face twisted and he groaned, "Radio? Radio is too hard!" His statement took me back, and I asked him what he meant. He told me that listening to radio requires you to sit still and imagine everything that is being said. "It is just too much hard work." I was speechless; radio too much work? What on earth would he do with poetry? If radio is too much work because it requires use of the imagination, what must he think of metaphor? In the end, he did the project. He shadowed a disk jockey on a local community radio station, and, as a result, fell in love with radio. Chalk up one victory for the imagination.

This exchange has stayed with me. Here was a bright, active 22-year-old getting ready to graduate from college, and he thought radio was too much work because it required him to use his imagination. Have we made everything too available to his generation? Have they seen too many slick, well-produced images on TV and computer screens? Do we give them too much that is already in finished form? Have they been invited to use their imagination, had it nurtured, had it challenged? I'm not sure that they don't want to use their imagination - I'm just not sure they know how powerful their imagination really is, or the innumerable ways in which metaphor is a part of their daily lives.

It isn't just some of our young people who are threatening the death of metaphor. I also know many adults who have difficulty dealing with metaphor. The more polarized we become, the less we seem to be able to communicate with each other. One reason is because we are too busy trying to convince people to think the way we do. In the process, we forget that language itself is a symbol, something that always points beyond itself. An example of a symbol is the United States flag. We know the flag stands for something - it points to our history, our heritage, our identity as a nation. It is a metaphor. A sign, on the other hand points only to itself . When we come to a stop sign, we know exactly what it means. We don't have to interpret, analyze, or think about it. We stop.

Some of what is happening in our polarized society is that symbol is becoming sign. When this happens, what is designed to point beyond itself (metaphor) becomes a noun, a thing - an object that is either worshiped (idolized) or despised (needing to be controlled or destroyed). Thinking of things as sign instead of symbol is easier, it requires less work because it doesn't require any imagination. The result of the loss of the imagination is the death of metaphor. And this potential death of metaphor may be the greatest crisis our nation will face in the next decade.

The Role of the Arts in Rebuilding the Front Porch of America

I have discussed two reasons why our communities are at risk. The first is because we don't have a gathering place, a front porch. The second is because we are losing the power of metaphor, the creative energy of the imagination. There is something that addresses both of these issues - it's called community arts.

Community arts are the new front porch of America. In community arts we invite people to gather together, much like our ancestors before us did; celebrating who we are as people in community, reclaiming and sharing our stories, and valuing our culture. In community arts, we also nurture the imagination, unlocking the creative potential of people of all ages. While this is not a common-place understanding of the role of the arts, it is one that is essential for us to understand if we are to fully understand the role of the arts in our personal lives and the life of our communities.

Community arts aren't about art as a sign - a noun, an object. They are about art as symbol - a verb, a process. Those of us engaged in community arts work understand our work is about creating a process that invites individuals to participate in and experience the arts on a personal basis. It is, in essence, a paradigm shift from "art as product and citizen as patron" to "art as process and citizen as participant." It is called community arts development. This is a very different orientation toward the arts and is not widely shared by our society. In fact, it is not always understood by the organizations and people with whom we work.

Community arts development is and always has been about relationships. It is people-oriented. It has a long and valued history of individuals taking the initiative to promote self-improvement through self-expression and self-education. Because of this, it has always had a process emphasis, a sensitivity to the way we do things. Those involved in community arts development recognize the way something is done is just as important, if not more important, than what it is we are doing. We live with the realization that the people with whom we work are the essential ingredients needed to insure our efforts are successful. These are the people who work and give of themselves, are often unrecognized for their efforts, and many times are unrealized in their self-image. This is especially true for those who live and work in rural and small communities. These are the people who do great things but many times think it could be done better by someone else, somewhere else, always thinking they aren't really gifted. And this negative self-image is very difficult to change. Yet we who do community arts development work, by choice or by the nature of our DNA, know the truth: we know these are the unrecognized geniuses, these people are the greatest natural resource our nation has to offer our communities.

It is this participation in and experience of the arts on a personal basis that connects community arts and community arts development to the process of rebuilding the front porch. Art is an invitation for people to tell their stories and to listen to the stories of others. Community arts experiences create places where people can gather together and celebrate their story as a community. Community arts experiences create circles of convergence where people can have a "common" experience. In this sense, art is very much a verb, an action word. It can be liked and disliked, but that isn't the same as being good or bad. Our tendency is to think of the art we like as being good and the art we don't like as being bad. When this happens, we miss the point of what art is really about.

What people involved in community arts development believe is that when we make art we are engaged in a community-making experience. The two are closely connected. They are connected because they engage people's imaginations in the act of self-expression (making art) and the act of community-making (sharing the art). This is what we have failed to communicate effectively to those around us. We have assumed all along that people understand what it is we are doing - that our community arts development work is part of the community-making process. Unfortunately, this isn't true. Very few people understand our work, including some of us who do it.

Those of us involved in community arts development have always faced this challenge in our work, especially in the rural and small community setting. But overcoming challenges has been what we do best. If we can see beyond the conflict and the challenge, we may discover that we are not at the end of community as we know it, but rather at the beginning of a community revival. We may not be experiencing the death of metaphor. Instead, we may be entering an era where the power of the imagination will be unleashed. But, for this to happen, we must take the long view. For too long we have been too narrowly focused on what is happening around us in the "here and now," and we have been ignoring the long view - the "then and there" of where we want to be years down the road. We have to address this cultural myopia and correct it. We can do this only with the long-view.

In a time of change and transition, art is a deep voice, authentically speaking to the reality of what is, and pointing to the possibility of what might be. It is for this reason, those of us involved in community arts development sometimes find ourselves at risk professionally and personally. It takes courage to speak the deep voice. It takes courage to challenge people with the power of metaphor. Art is not always beautiful. Creating art is not always easy. There can be pain attached to this process, and we live in a society that more readily denies pain than faces it.

People who deny pain will use art as an "an-esthetic." They promote the role of art as something to dull the pain and provide an escape. This is art as noun; art as a product that has little depth. It is not authentic. It is not the deep voice, because it originates from the surface of our lives; the shallow place that is safe and comfortable. On the other hand, there is art as verb; art as a process that is vibrant. It is full of pain but it is also full of joy. It is full of reality but it is also full of possibility. This is understanding art as a process that invites all of us to discover and express what it means to be fully human. This is community arts development. But the context in which it occurs is undergoing constant change. To understand this dynamic, we have to look at the changing inscape of our rural and small communities.

The Changing Inscape of Our Communities

The first part of this essay provides a glimpse into the changing inscape and transforming cultural ecology facing our rural and small communities. These are just a few of the challenges communities face. The causes of our cultural conflicts are deeply rooted - they are not likely to go away anytime soon. To contribute to the future of our communities, we must not only identify the problems, but find creative ways to resolve them. Acknowledging that the front porch of America is in disrepair is not enough. We must do more than show how the front porch of America is in disrepair. We have to show people how the arts can help rebuild the front porch. There are several changes on the horizon that promise to have tremendous impact on how we go about doing this. Let us look at just a few.

Agriculture of the Heart

We need to realize the deep hunger people have to become "makers" again. We have become a nation of consumers, a people defined by the consumption of things made by others. As a result, we have little relationship between the things we use/consume and the people who make them. This has created a market-place, commodity-based society. We have also lost our contact with the earth and the environment around us. Someone else does the farming, the growing. We have become disconnected from the agricultural tradition that historically defined many of our rural and small communities. Some believe this is one of the reasons we are facing the current ecological crisis. When we moved from an agrarian society to an industrial age, we set in motion an alienation from that which had provided sustenance and meaning for centuries - the land. We are now beginning to experience the full impact of this loss of relationship with our environment. People are beginning to realize they miss growing things, they miss making things.

The arts provide us with an opportunity to become "makers" again, not just consumers. The arts invite us to create, and in the process, re-value the worth of the everyday things in our life we frequently take for granted. Becoming art-makers enhances our aesthetic sensibilities. When we participate in the creative process of making, we can discover our own personal creative power. We can also discover the power of being involved in a creative environment and the contribution it makes to our "sense of community." This can happen both in the process of making art and making art happen for others. When this occurs, people not only discover they can become makers again, they realize they can make a difference in their community. This is one of the core values driving community arts development work. People are hungry for a sense of community again. They know something is missing and they want it back. When we connect this to the desire people have to become "makers" again, we may see the beginning of a new kind of agrarian society, focusing on the creative process of cultivating the intra personal and interpersonal relationships associated with this new community. Those of us involved in community arts development can provide the invitation for people to engage in this "agriculture of the heart," nurturing and growing who we are as a people, as a community. People want to make again. And they want to feel they make a difference, that what they do matters. Community arts development provides an opportunity for these to happen.

The New Community

Changing demographics will also have a dramatic effect on our communities. The nature of work is undergoing (or has already undergone) enormous transformation. We are rapidly reaching the point in time when we will no longer be defined by the work we do. The way we look at our work and the kind of work we do continues to change as well. People are pointing to the rise of the private, nonprofit, independent sector as an essential opportunity for participation in a new kind of work - community service. This provides a growing area in which people will be looking for an opportunity to volunteer their time and make a contribution to their community. This may also become the sector in which people will be looking to find paid employment. There are several demographic changes that promise to have a tremendous influence on our communities, especially our rural and small communities.

A. Re-Valuing Our Elders

Those in the older generation, currently retirement age, are leaving their metropolitan nests and looking for smaller communities to live out the rest of their lives. A brand new source of volunteers is moving into communities just at the time when we are experiencing our greatest depletion of our volunteer pool. It may actually compensate for the loss of the more traditional volunteer pool, previously consisting of young mothers who are now working and no longer able to volunteer the same amount of time. These older citizens (the wealth-holders in our society), have a strong sense of organizational loyalty and are accustomed to supporting non-profit, community organizations. They are highly skilled, frequently well-educated, and will be looking for ways to become involved in their new communities. This generation is one of the most exciting resources to come to rural and small communities in decades.

Unfortunately there is a long-standing bias we have against age in our culture. We are going to have to face it and overcome it. The de-valuing of our elders in our society is one of the major contributors to the loss of our sense community in our culture. Historically, our elders have been the story tellers. With ageism the way it is in our current society, we pay little attention to our elders. In the process, we have lost contact not only with our story, but our storytellers as well. They not only know the stories, they are the ones who grew up with the tradition of storytelling. They grew up on the front porch, listening to their older relatives tell the family and community stories. Our elders can be the teachers of many generations, modeling not only the importance of story in our lives, but also the role of volunteer service in our communities.

Our community arts agencies can be a beneficiary of this new volunteer pool. These elders are the people who grew up believing that art was an important part of their lives. These are the people who believe it is their job to support the arts, both financially and individually. These are the people who will work hard to reinstate the arts to their important role in the life of the community in which they live.

My parents fit into this category. Our family was never involved in the arts as I grew up. And we lived less than thirty minutes from one of the most culturally active and diverse cities in the country, San Francisco. I don't remember going to an arts event once as I grew up as a child. When my parents retired, they returned to the small community environment in which they were raised in the San Joaquin Valley in central California. The first thing they did when they moved was to buy season tickets to the local community theatre. They became involved in supporting the work of nonprofit organizations and enjoyed the opportunity to make a contribution. When I asked them why the sudden interest in the arts (somewhat surprised at their apparent change of heart), they said they had always been interested in the arts. They just didn't want the hassle of having to deal with it in a large city. They didn't have the time and the energy. When they retired, they did.

B. Seeking the Simple Life - Discovering Simple/Complexity

Baby boomers are beginning to look for a simpler way of life. They are tired of the demands their work and their lifestyle are making on them. In essence, they are engaging in what some are calling a personal "voluntary downsizing." They are not finding meaning in their work. Many, just now reaching fifty, are walking away from traditional paths of success and professional advancement in search of something else. One of the reasons they are leaving their work is because this generation has never had a strong sense of corporate/organizational loyalty. The other reason is they want their lives to be different. They don't just want to work -

they want to make a difference with their work. To accomplish these goals, some are deciding to move to rural and small communities in quest of what they perceive to be a less complicated life, a more simple lifestyle. While not the same wealth-holders as their retiring parents, many do have enough financial security to enable them to make these changing lifestyle decisions.

Once they find their new community, they will soon discover life in rural and small communities is not quite as "simple" as they thought. Life in rural and small communities consists of a rather complex maze of cultural rules and norms. Community doesn't happen because you live there. Community happens because we make conscious, intentional decisions to make it happen. For many of this generation - experts at cacooning and disengagement - this will require a tremendous change. It will require a commitment and willingness to become involved. Facing this new challenge, their temptation may be to continue the comfort of their big city ways, including keeping to themselves. If they are not engaged in a community, they cannot be a part of it and this defeats the purpose of living in a small community setting.

Even if they do want to make a connection with their new communities, they may not know how. Community arts can provide them with opportunities to make the community connection they are looking for. They may also provide a way for them to contribute their time and energy to the community, becoming part of something that is making a difference in a lot of people's lives. Being involved in the creative process of self-expression and the community-making activities of the arts can help them make this adjustment and find a meaningful place in the new community they are now helping to create. When they find the balance between their individual needs and the needs of the community, they will discover the simple-complexity of rural and small communities. In the process, they may just find what they have been looking for - a way to add meaning to their lives and make a difference at the same time.

C. Creating the Terminal Community

People will soon choose the community in which they live because they want to live there, not because of the work they do. They will do this because of the development of the "virtual office." The information and technology revolution makes it possible for people to no longer have to rely on the community in which they live to make a living. Until the development of the "virtual office," the only people previously able to do this were those individuals who were independently wealthy.

Many of these people will live, by choice, in rural and small communities. They can do this because their work will be unaffected by the economic resources available to them where they live. Their technologically-outfitted office will overcome any historical economic barriers that living in rural and small communities has presented in the past. They can live in a community and never have their work affected by it. These "terminal communities" will consist of many people whose work is totally disconnected from the community in which they live - people who instead, will be plugged into a larger, national/global network. This promises to bring a whole new kind of diversity to communities of all sizes. The challenge will be to find a way to connect these virtual office workers to the community in which they have chosen to live - since their work has no connection to the place or people of the community in which they are living. Wherever there is "high tech" there will be an increased need for "high touch." Community arts can provide this important human network that will plug these "terminal community commuters" into the traditional human community in which they live. These people will be looking for ways to enter the community and become part of it. Participation in the nonprofit, community-service sector can provide an excellent entry point into the broader community. At the same time, their participation in these organizations can give them a way to interact with this community, becoming part of it. This is especially true for the community arts experiences available to them.

Summary

If these demographic trends continue, they will present a challenge to every community affected by them - the challenge of learning to live with change. Communities must be open to the changes and the different values these changes will bring into the existing culture. Communities must preserve the essence of who they are as a community and still be open to the change surrounding them. This is not an easy balance to maintain, but it is necessary if these communities are to survive and have a future. If they aren't successful these communities will become even more isolated than they are now. At best, they will struggle with the change and be uncomfortable with it. At the worst, they will be charting a course toward cultural isolation, eventually becoming the wrong kind of "terminal community."

Historically, rural and small communities have not been noted for being open to change and to new people. For that matter, they have not always been open to new ideas. Those who were involved in the rural migration of the mid-1970s learned this lesson very early on. This new rural migration promises much more substantial and sustained impact on rural and small communities. As this migration occurs, the single largest issue facing everyone will be that of cultural diversity. We must understand that diversity is not just an issue of color, but also of race, religion, age, gender, economics, and much more. The changing demographics of our communities indicates a change in all of these categories. With this in mind, cultural diversity can't be brushed aside, being viewed only as a social mandate for "political correctness." Honoring and valuing our diversity is an essential element of being part of the human community.

Addressing the importance of diversity and understanding how integral it is to our future enables us to have a future. Those of us working in the rural and small community environment need to recognize the gift and potential of this cultural diversity as the most powerful element of our changing cultural ecology. We must find new strategies and resources to share this understanding with the communities we serve. Those of us involved in community arts development can provide our communities with a mechanism and a means to address these changes and challenges. We may be in the best position to help our communities find creative ways to be in control of the change, to become change masters.

We are standing at the threshold of a whole new kind of human community. Instead of looking at what we have lost or what we are losing, we can use our imaginations, take the initiative, and be engaged in the creative process of rebuilding the front porch of America.

Nurturing the Invisible Culture
of Rural Genius

The arts are an invitation. They invite us to tell our stories and they invite us to listen to the stories of those around us. They also invite us to celebrate who we are together. In rural and small communities all across our country, community arts provide a new gathering place, a cultural and spiritual touchstone that is a source of community revitalization and neighborhood revival. In a way, you could say community arts have become the new front porch of America.

There is one thing and one thing only of which I am clear: we are living in a time of change and transition. Nothing we know is, or will stay, the same. It is not only that things have changed, what has changed we know will end up changing again. We are a society marked by uncertainty. What does this mean for those of us who work in rural and small communities? Should we be working to help these communities address the changes that have already occurred? Or should we encourage and promote further change in these communities? Is it one or the other? Or could it be both?

Community arts development in rural and small communities is different and we have not always understood these differences. Those of us who work in the rural and small community context don't necessarily believe it is a "better way of life." What we do know is that it is a different way of life. This essay is about identifying these differences. It is also about what I consider to be the most unique and important aspect of community arts development - its role in nurturing the invisible culture of rural genius.

The Invisible Culture

In the United States, rural and small communities have always had a specific purpose. Their citizens dug the coal needed to create energy to electrify a nation; mined the minerals locked in rock and stone required to fuel a growing American industrial skyline; harvested the trees of our forests to provide lumber for houses and shelter for millions of families; and farmed the land to grow food for consumption to feed not only a hungry nation, but a world as well. They cleared the wilderness and pioneered a new nation into existence. From the beginning, they harvested their natural resources and sent them away to an ever-growing concentration of people in crowded metropolitan locations, mostly located in the eastern portion of the United States. This was how they made their living. They worked with their hands and the work of their hands sustained our nation. It was a simple life consisting of hard, but meaningful work that returned to them a sense of pride and personal satisfaction.

People in rural and small communities were connected to the land and understood they were in relationship with the earth. These early pioneer citizens knew they were stewards of the land.

And, they knew what the rest of us are just beginning to find out-you can't "manage" rivers - they will rise and wipe out all controls and restrictions imposed upon them; you can't mine resources without accepting the impact this has on the land and the lives of those who live on it; and you can't keep using the land without depleting its strength and reducing its yield. They knew this and, for the most part, they lived by these rules.

This is the invisible culture of rural America. It is a culture that people who live outside these communities do not understand. People who visit this culture sense it but don't really get a chance to experience it, unless it is marketed as a product under the name of "traditional art" and taken out of the community context in which it was created. Even those who live in it, and whose lives are shaped by it, don't always see it. Perhaps it is too much with them. Some people in rural and small communities do see it and they are embarrassed by it, or feel it is inferior to the culture other communities have, and do their best to hide it. They have bought into the belief that little good can come from rural and small communities. The more geographically isolated the community is, the more likely it is this attitude exists.

Whatever the reason, the fact is, no one has really made a fuss about this invisible culture before. It was just there. It was part of the day-to-day lives of its people. It was taken for granted. It didn't have a name because it didn't need one. Unfortunately, as a result of this, it seems this culture is not only invisible, it has begun to disappear as other, outside cultural values work their way into our daily lives. The invisible culture of rural and small communities is at risk and people in these communities are engaged in a struggle for the very existence of their communities. It is a struggle facing almost every rural and small community in the United States.

The Invisible Culture in Crisis

As I listen to people in rural and small communities speak, it is evident from what they say and the intensity with which they are saying it, something is wrong. They know something is wrong but they don't know what it is. They know their community has changed but they can't identify how. They know they are uncomfortable with the change but they can't quite put their finger on what it is that bothers them and causes their discomfort. They feel they are being forced to make choices, but they don't understand the choices and they don't understand why they have to make them.

There are numerous contributing factors to the existence of this invisible culture. First of all, many rural and small communities came into existence in geographically isolated areas. In fact, geography defined their existence - that is why they were created. The people who lived in these communities relied on themselves for education, entertainment, and enjoyment. They spent time together. Everyone knew each other's name. Neighbors were considered extended family, and shared in the rites, rituals, and responsibilities of raising children. The communities had their own traditions, history, and stories, but they didn't have names for all of this. The terms culture, values, and art, didn't have names because they were considered part of the everyday lives of the people in these communities. They were not objectified and set apart from the daily context of their existence. Their culture was woven into their lives as effortlessly and tirelessly as the quilts stitched by mothers and grandmothers that kept them warm in the deepest cold of the most bitter winters. They didn't need to have a name for it. The fact it was there was enough.

The intent of this description is not to paint an idyllic existence of pastoral beauty and perfection. Anyone who believes this doesn't understand the nature and reality of living in rural and small community America. Life in rural and small communities is anything but perfection. It is anything but easy. Living in these communities has always demanded a strong survival instinct. But many people who lived in these communities embodied the two driving American pioneer values - rugged individualism and a strong sense of community. While seemingly contradictory values, successful rural and small communities were able to create a balance between these two extremes. They created the common sense and the common place that enabled these values not only to co-exist but to thrive. The determination and will of the individual was absolutely paramount to survival in these geographically isolated areas. Yet, when this individualism was put into the context of the larger community setting, it provided the companionship and shared resources that helped them survive. It was the best of both worlds. It let them keep their independence, but, at the same time, celebrate the interdependence of being in community.

But, when the world began to lose its balance between individualism and community, it affected the invisible culture of rural and small communities. Communities, though still geographically isolated, were suddenly invaded by another world, the world outside the invisible boundaries of their invisible culture. The advancement of technologies and communication media has not only brought everything closer to them, it actually placed the whole world on their front porch. As a result, it was also forced into their daily lives and the lives of their children. This world and its culture was not the same as the one in which they were raised. And increasingly, there has been no place to escape this intrusion. This invasion of the outside world and its changing values has been quiet, slow, but it has been consistent. It has been called progress and touted as that which brings people together. Unfortunately, its impact in rural and small communities created a silent and unseen transformation of almost everything they value, understand, live and work for, and want to pass on to their children.

Because of this, the invisible culture of many of these communities has begun to disappear. Older people are losing touch with their "grassroots" and find themselves in the middle of a world that is both confusing and uncomfortable. Younger people find themselves untethered and afraid, uncertain of the future. The end result is what could be called an "erosion" of cultural values. As it occurs, people have gradually lost their ability to control, conserve, celebrate, and transmit the values they inherited as individuals and as members of a larger community. They no longer feel able to serve as stewards of the land they received from their parents because the control of the land has been taken away from them. They no longer feel they are the keepers of the stories because there are other voices telling other stories. The corner grocery story and local cafe coffee klatch are replaced by quick stops and fast food franchises. The clock speeds up, we move faster, and indeed, the world beyond the boundaries of their invisible culture is "too much with them." Soon, they begin to forget what makes them special, no longer remembering why they live where they live. And there are those outside the physical boundaries of these rural and small communities who have begun a second "rural migration," moving to what they consider to be more sane and acceptable places. Unfortunately, they bring with them their other world and other worldly expectations, including all of their fears and mistrust. For people who live in rural and small communities, there is both a "knowing" and a "gnawing." It is a knowing that something is wrong, and a gnawing that there is nothing they can do about it. And this makes them afraid.

The culture external to rural and small communities, much of which promotes values that are contradictory to those values that have been the foundation of rural and small community life for over three hundred years, is finding its way into our towns, our schools, our families, and our personal lives. We can't escape it. It is projected into our living rooms through television, channeled into the ears of our "walkman" teenagers, and put on the big screen in front of all of us. It is there and we can't avoid it - this world is "way too much with us."

One thing we do know is that our children seem to learn more about values from television, film, and music, than they are from their family and neighbors. And these values are in conflict with the community values we have relied upon for so long. In addition, drive-by shootings, car-jackings, gang violence, drug dealers, alcoholism in teenagers, and sexually transmitted diseases, are becoming part of our daily conversations. These aren't descriptions of horrible things happening in those "other" places - they are descriptions of where we live now - it is a description of our own rural or small communities. Our national cultural fabric is stretched, its edges are frayed, and the threads are unraveling. The world as we know it has changed and we are afraid there is nothing we can do to stop it.

The Invisible Culture of Rural Genius

In the midst of the fear and the discomfort, there is something else that exists in the invisible culture of rural and small communities that we need to acknowledge. There is something special in people in rural and small communities - it is one of America's most valuable natural resources - "rural genius." It is that special resource that turned the wilderness into thriving communities. It is still there, and it is a powerful source of energy but it largely remains hidden, unknown, undiscovered - and something needs to be done to unleash this untapped natural resource.

One of the most important natural resources we have in this country is that of rural genius. It has been the fuel that has driven the development of this country from the moment the first native American walked the ground, and the first Puritan set foot on our soil. It is the creativeness and innovation that has brought into existence the society in which we now live. Rural genius has been raised and nurtured in communities all across America and the arts have been a vital part of this. But this rural genius is at risk. This natural resource is being depleted as our young people continue to leave the communities and not return. The farm crisis and subsequent economic hardship has contributed to the struggle of rural and small communities to survive.

The Role of the Arts in Nurturing the Invisible Culture of Rural Genius

The challenge facing all of us who work in rural and small communities is to help people find a way to address and overcome their fear and nurture rural genius at the same time. Community arts are one of the ways we can do both. The community arts experience provides an opportunity to overcome the sense of isolation and separation that is one of the causes of people's fear. Community arts bring people together, the way they used to gather on the front porch. The arts inspire, reveal, renew. The arts help promote creative thinking and self-expression.

Community arts create a new gathering place, a means of neighborhood revival, a cultural touchstone that is a source of community revitalization. It is multi-cultural and inter-generational, cutting across traditional socio-economic barriers, bringing people together who would not otherwise be working toward the same goal. It is not limited to the concert hall, the stage, or the art conservatories. It is ever present in the public schools, the PTA, the Senior Citizens' Centers, recreation programs, art leagues, community theatres, choirs, and more. It permeates every level of community life, for the arts in rural and small communities are integrated into the everyday lives of their citizens. It is not just an event to which they go, it is something they do and the way they do it. Art is a way of life for many people in these communities and it is becoming more and more this way all across America. Community arts administrators are no longer individuals who just manage facilities and negotiate contracts with artists. Terms such as cultural diversity, community liveability, cultural tourism, community cultural planning, community organizing, economic development, and downtown revitalization are just a few to describe the ways in which their jobs have changed. These are also words that describe the way in which the arts are changing the inscape of rural America. The term is "community arts development." There were people long before us who realized that the arts can be a creative process that challenges and changes individuals and communities.   Many people have spent years making this process a reality in the rural and small communities they served. This same vision is alive in many people today.

The arts are a way of remembering the story of our invisible culture. It is a way of giving a name to that which was always nameless. And by giving it a name, it allows people who live in these communities to identify it as something they want to keep, something they have to keep. Cultural organizations all across our country are working to identify and preserve this invisible culture. Art is story and it is an invitation for people to tell their story and to listen to the story of others. It is based on the dual value of process and product - it is a constantly changing balance between the two. It is a process that reveals and it is a product that invites others to share in this revelation. The balance between process and product helps us understand our relationship with everything else around us.

By the very nature of art, it is an invitation for the creation of common ground - circles of convergence that invite people to gather and share. It invites people to learn to be together and not have to be the same or think the same way. In this way, the arts are one of the essential ways in which cultural values are identified, conserved, celebrated, and transmitted. It is this, one of the more unique aspects of art, that I find most intriguing and fascinating. This is also why I believe the presence and vitality of the arts in a community setting is so essential to the growth and perhaps even the continuation of that community of people. It recognizes that when an individual participates in and experiences the arts on a personal basis, it not only changes that person, but it sets in motion a series of indirect influences that has an impact on the community as a whole.

As wonderful as all of this sounds, the reality is that our communities are full of people who do not understand this. One of the reasons for this is that our communities are full of people who are "art scarred" and "art scared." The art scarred are those who had some negative experience early on (usually an art teacher of some kind) that has stuck with them their entire life and made them hate the arts. Then there are the art scared, those were told early on that art was so profound, so important, so beyond them, they could never understand it. So they don't bother. Our communities consist of both of these kinds of people. Overcoming being art scarred is not easy. Overcoming being art scared can be even more difficult. But this is the real challenge facing us. Part of our task in community arts development is to own up to this reality and try and do something to change it. There are thousands of stories that can demonstrate the power of community arts development to accomplish this task. Here is one of them.

Greg's Story

It used to be that when people asked me where I was from, I told them I grew up in the San Francisco Bay Area. After 8 ½ years as director of the Boonville Community Arts Program, I now answer the question by saying I was raised in the San Francisco Bay Area - I grew up in Boonville, Missouri.

The work I did during that time was some of the most rewarding, challenging, stimulating, and sometimes exasperating work of my life. When I think of my work in Boonville, I think of people. I think of the people with whom I worked. I think of some of the people with whom I disagreed. But most of all, I think of the people whose lives were changed by what we did in creating that program.

I remember one person in particular. His name was Greg. He was the son of a grocery store owner. He had a good singing voice. It was a natural voice, but not well-developed. He was in his late twenties and used his voice mostly for weddings and funerals. But he had always wanted to be on stage. We made the decision to do a musical. It seemed this was the best way to get everyone in the arts involved together for one project. We chose the musical "Bye Bye Birdie" and Greg was cast in the lead role of Conrad Birdie. But he had great difficulty. Up to this point, he had always been able to get along on a good voice by using a microphone. But now he not only had to project, he had to take on a very different character than he had ever been before. In other words, he had to act. And it was hard. He was very self-conscious and I was asking him to really let loose on stage and take on a totally new, wild persona. One evening a few weeks into rehearsal, he finally stopped mid-song and said he just couldn't do it. He quit. The rehearsal was obviously over. I sent everyone home but Greg. I asked him to stay.

I locked the door to the theater and went back inside. As I walked down the aisle, toward the stage, I confided in him something that no one else involved with the production knew. I surprised him by telling him I had never directed a musical before and that he had no more fear of failure than I did. I challenged him to own up to what was really going on, which was his fear of taking a risk - of risking failure. We argued, we struggled, and we shared. In the process, we created a partnership - we agreed that we would do it together. There was a lot riding on the success of the show, and we both decided it was worth the risk. That evening changed both of our lives. I honestly believe it changed the life of our community as well.

Greg eventually reached inside, found his character, and gave a tremendous performance. He actually became Conrad Birdie. I'll never forget that first time when the character of Conrad arrived on stage. It was during a rehearsal and it was magical. At the time of the production, Boonville, Missouri, was a community of 6,500 people. During the three performances of the musical, over 1,800 of them saw the show. It was, without question, one of the most exciting things to happen in that town for years. I count my experience with that theatrical production as one of the highlights of my life. We overcame insurmountable odds and did what many people in the community didn't think we could do. And, most of the time, we had fun doing it. This was the beginning of our rebuilding the front porch of Boonville. It set in motion a community transformation that can still be felt today, twenty years later.

Greg and I never talked about that evening's rehearsal and subsequent encounter between the two of us. We became very good friends, and I directed Greg one more time in "The Wizard of Oz" (he was the Lion and a magnificent one at that). To this day, I consider him one of the most gifted performers with whom I have worked in musical theatre. And there is no question his experience with this production set in motion changes in his personal and professional life. He did not give up his small town life to seek the lights of Broadway. He didn't need to. He found the lights on the stage of Thespian Hall and that was enough.

When I prepared to leave my position seven years later and go back to school to work on my Ph.D., I happened by the grocery store where Greg worked one evening just before it closed. I was reaching into the freezer to get a pint of ice cream. It was a corner freezer and I had to face the open door and reach in sideways to get what I wanted. Just as I was about to reach that pint of ice cream, my face against the freezer door, I suddenly felt a physical presence next to me. It was Greg. He had me blocked in - I couldn't move. He leaned in very close to me and very quietly said, "You changed my life, and I will never forget you." By the time I could get my arm out of the freezer and turn around, he was gone.

I will never forget that moment. Of all the experiences I have had in my work as a community maker, I am not sure I have ever been moved quite as much as I was then. The fact is, I didn't change Greg's life, I helped create the opportunity for him to change his own life. He chose to accept the invitation. This is community arts development! This is community-making at its best - one person at a time. If you develop the individual you invite the development of the whole community. If you heal the heart - you heal the whole person. If you believe in people - and give them the opportunity - they will discover their creative gifts. When this happens, it is a powerful force to behold. It is the power of rural genius.

Surviving the Values Collision

I will never forget a Missouri Arts Council public meeting I attended when I was Director of the Missouri Association of Community Arts Agencies. It was a panel meeting to determine what community arts agencies would receive funding through the state agency's Community Arts Program. One of the Council members on the panel made quite a few critical comments regarding several of the grant proposals, raising questions about quality and issues relating to the "criteria of excellence" they were to focus on in their review of the applications. Addressing one application that was requesting a small amount of money for a community theatre production, she finally said in a frustrated and anguished voice, "But, is this the kind of art we want in this community?" It wasn't what she said that caught those of us sitting in the audience off guard. What surprised us was that she had said it out loud, in a public meeting. We knew she operated from a value system that was different from those of us who work with and live in rural and small communities. Those of us in community arts development have dealt with this "values collision" for years. She was not a mean-spirited person and I do not believe she meant to be condescending. She honestly believed her responsibility was to ensure our communities had "good art" and to her, good art had to be imported into rural and small communities because people in these communities weren't capable of producing it themselves. The fact is, some of the most professional quality art I have seen has been produced by "non-paid professionals" in rural and small communities.

There is a war going on. It is a cultural and religious war the likes of which we have not seen since the 1950's. War was officially declared by Pat Buchanan at the 1992 Republican convention, but it had its start hundreds of years ago when the first Europeans landed on the North American continent. It is a war about values - about whose values will prevail and about whose values will be denied. It is a war that forces people to take sides. As a result of this, everything we have been working for the past twenty years, all of the community making we have been doing, and all of our efforts to help people understand the role of the arts in our lives, is at risk. Will the arts community as we know it survive? Perhaps the more important question is whether or not the communities we serve will survive.

The Problem

Our communities are in trouble. We are in the middle of one of the most intense cultural wars this country has seen since the civil war. Perhaps the term "Uncivil War" is a better description. And it is a war our entire country is waging, and at the present time, losing. It is a war about values - about whose values will prevail - and about whose values will be denied. It is a war that forces people to take sides - families, communities, regions. Not since the Civil War has the cultural fabric of this nation been so much at risk of tearing apart at the seams. And it threatens to leave in its wake, communities wounded by its confrontive and combative nature. The reason the arts are in trouble is because our communities are in trouble. We don't know how to talk to each other any more. We don't know how to disagree and still be in relationship with each other. We have lost our ability to communicate with each other. Simply put, we seem to have lost our "common ground" and one of the reasons for this is we have lost our "common courtesy."

This cultural war isn't about public funding for art or even the role of art in our communities - these are just symptoms of a larger problem. The battle we are fighting is for the heart and soul of our nation. And you and I, by some strange quirk of fate, community makers by choice or by circumstance, find ourselves caught in the crossfire of this cultural and religious war. We have ended up smack in the middle of one of the greatest values collisions this nation has ever experienced. Everything we have been working for over the past twenty years, all of the community cultural building we have been doing, and all of our efforts to help people understand the role of the arts in our everyday lives, is at risk. What some people propose as clear-cut choices to solve our social problems, others see as creating problems of their own. Many of us struggle because we are less sure of what side to take. Or we see right and wrong in both sides. This is not a popular position because we live in a time of polarization that requires people to take one side or another.

To further complicate the situation, those of us in community arts work many times find ourselves and our values not only in conflict with those outside the arts community, but also within the arts community itself. Sometimes we are in conflict with the very organizations and individuals with which we work and serve. This is the ethical dilemma those of us involved in community arts development deal with every day. And it has taken a tremendous toll on all of us. We have been sidetracked from our work, lured away from the vision that drives us, diverted by the intensity of the cultural conflict surrounding us. The fact is, most of us in the arts don't have much energy left. We have had to mount too many emergency campaigns, conduct too many advocacy efforts just to survive. We are tired and frustrated, and if we are honest, most of us are angry. Someone else has been setting our agenda. And worst of all, those of us involved in the arts have been branded as promoters of pornography and obscenity; attacking the very heart and soul of our work. While this attack has primarily manifested at the national level, it is starting to materialize in our own local communities. First in our school boards, then our libraries, and increasingly, the arts in the community. We are exhausted. We need a rest.

It is time to come home. Time to come back to the home place and sit on the porch for a while. It's time to remember why we do what we do. We have been neglecting it - we have been neglecting ourselves. We have become too concerned with getting the grants and too concerned with creating the programs to get the grants to make up for the grants we aren't getting. We have been side-tracked from the values that drive our work.

I do not consider myself a pessimist. I have always considered myself a problem-solver. But increasingly, I find myself engaged in less "community-making" activities and more "community-sustaining" efforts. Rather than working with organizations and communities to move forward, I am spending all of my time trying to help them cut the losses and preserve what growth has already occurred. It isn't just because there isn't enough money; there has never been enough money and that hasn't stopped us before. It isn't because people don't like the art we are doing. There are always people who don't like the art we are doing. It is because people do not understand why we are doing art - and I'm not sure that the majority of our population has ever understood the role the arts play in our communities. We have no one to blame for this but ourselves. After twenty years of concerted, intense effort to promote community-based art, we have failed to communicate the reason why we are promoting art in the first place. Most of our efforts have been to Congress and state legislatures. We have paid little attention to communicating the value of the arts to the very communities of people we serve. Without their support and understanding, it doesn't matter how much money and resources we bring in from outside the community - we won't be successful. We won't reach the people we want to serve. Unless we begin to communicate our arguments for the arts more effectively, the arts may well be one of the casualties of the cultural and religious war being waged in communities all across our nation. In the end, the real losers will be the people and the communities in which they live.

Overcoming the "Enemy" Mentality

I attended a meeting a few years ago in Washington DC. The people gathered in the room were some of the most articulate and respected community arts leaders in the country. It was a very frustrating meeting. The talk centered around what appeared to be the imminent demise of the National Endowment for the Arts. We were witnessing the undoing of over twenty-five years of our life's work and the frustration level in the room was high. It wasn't long before we moved into the "war talk," with people in the room identifying the evangelical religious and political right as the "enemies" responsible for all our problems. The people gathered in the room talked about the cultural war, and the strategies we had to create to defeat the enemy and win this battle for the hearts and minds of our nation. The problem with this kind of talk is that it doesn't solve the problem, it increases the level of confrontation. The other problem with this is the people who are part of the evangelical religious and political right aren't our enemies, they are our audience. These are the ones who buy tickets to our community theatre performances. These are the ones who volunteer for our organizations and contribute their time and money to causes in which they believe. These are the citizens of the communities we serve. The point is that every community has people who share these beliefs. We can't ignore them, we have to find a way to communicate with them. Besides, there isn't one of us who works in the arts who is any less evangelical, any less intense, any less determined to communicate our message. The only difference is those in the religious and political right seem to be more clear and articulate about the values upon which their beliefs are based. And they are determined to communicate these values every chance they get.

There are many people in rural and small communities who care deeply about their community and their country. They have a value system that is very conservative and traditional. They place a high value on their religious beliefs and do not separate them out from their every day lives. And there is a growing sense these people have that we are losing our values as a nation. They can see it in their day-to-day lives. For many of these people, this results in the fear discussed earlier in this book. And the fear mentality produces confrontation. There must be something or someone of which we are afraid - there must be an enemy. It is easier to demonize people than it is to listen to them. It is easier to think of art as a sign rather than a symbol. And when art is viewed as a sign, it can be objectified, turned into a noun. And a noun is a thing that can be destroyed, or stopped. So, in a strange way, many people in the evangelical religious and political right have confused the values some art communicates with the role the arts play in communicating cultural values. Some think if the "nasty and negative" art is stopped, our values will be protected and preserved. Unfortunately, the fallacy in this thinking is that art is not a noun, it is not a sign. Art is a symbol, pointing to something else. By not seeing art as a symbol, many people lose the real message the arts are communicating. This is the death of metaphor of which I spoke about in the opening essay. It is easy to point to what the arts are saying and be upset. It is a lot harder to listen to the message the arts are sending and determine to do something about it. It is also easier for some people to support art that is "an-esthetic" than it is to support art that challenges our attitudes and values, provokes our emotions, and yes, perhaps even offends our sensibilities.

So here we are - a society full of people who are unhappy and angry with what we see going on around us. The evangelical religious and political right sees the arts and artists as a cause of social disintegration because they believe there is no regard for traditional values. They also believe people involved in the arts have no sense of community responsibility. On the other hand, many people involved in the arts have stereotyped all people involved in evangelical religious and political right as promoters of censorship. They see them as cultural zealots who sacrifice freedom of expression in order to protect the values they hold dear. They believe people who are conservative and religious have no interest in individual rights. And, then there are the rest of us, exactly where we usually are - right in the middle between the two. There is no right or wrong here - there are just different value systems in operation. One value system sees art as symbol-metaphor. The other side sees art as sign-object. And neither side really knows the values driving the other side. This is because we don't know how to communicate with people who disagree with us. And we end up doing the only thing we are really good at: making enemies of those we do not know or understand and treating them accordingly.

The battle over the arts is only one of the issues with which this is happening, but it is certainly one that has generated a lot of attention. The arts seem to have become a magnet for the confrontation and controversy that riddles our society. This will increasingly be the case. The problem with a values collision is that values are invisible. They are evident only as seen in relation to someone's action and action leaves a lot open to interpretation.

What is the Values Collision?

Needless to say, we have a major problem and it is a little more complicated than most people believe. First, there are the major arts and cultural institutions that will suffer enormously with the loss of public funding. Their budgets have been underwritten by public funding dollars for years and little has been done to replace what is now being lost. Some of these larger institutions will not survive. They have been dependent upon public funding for too long. The audience they serve is small and sometimes disproportionate to the public monies they have been receiving. These are the more traditional, Eurocentric art disciplines of symphony, opera, and dance.

Second, there is the evangelical religious and political right. This consists of people in our communities who are deeply concerned about one of the greatest spiritual crises our nation has ever faced. Unfortunately, many of them are unable to separate the values the arts represent from the way the arts represent these values. There is a failure to understand art as symbol that points beyond itself. There is a kind of "mythic literal" approach to art that defines it as a sign, something that points only to itself - a thing, an object. And they honestly believe if you destroy what it is that is the object of the evil, you are destroying the evil itself.

Third, there are the individual artists who not only believe that public funding is important, but something to which they have a right. Many of these people also believe they have no obligation to the public that gives them the money. To them, art is a process of making a political statement and the paramount issue facing them is freedom of expression. To them, the loss of public funding is a kind of censorship. Much of the time, this approach to art ends up being little more than propaganda, taking on the role of art as sign, very much like many of the people who are opposed to art because they think it is evil.

Finally, there are many of us involved in the community arts movement, who believe the real issue isn't the right to public funding or freedom of expression - it is our failure to effectively communicate the real value of the arts to the general public. While we recognize the role of the arts as individual expression, we also recognize the essential relationship this has to the community as a whole. For us, the issue to be addressed is individuals having access to the opportunity for self-expression. Public funding can help make this possible, but we serve a constituency in community arts that has historically not been served effectively by public funding. The loss of public funding won't destroy community arts. The real problem is the people in our communities who do not understand the values driving our work in community arts development. We have to start paying attention to the "home place," tend to the home fires. We need to do a better job of communicating with the people we serve.

Reconciling these different and, sometimes, opposing value systems is not going to be an easy thing to do. There is no easy way out of this dilemma. What we have going on is value systems colliding with each other. And, because we have failed to identify the issues facing us as a conflict of values, we continue to engage in battle after battle of a cultural war that hardly anyone understands. If it continues, the culture of our entire nation will become a casualty.

Community Arts and the Values Collision

To look at these value collisions, it is helpful to put it into a larger context. Let's examine three overarching values collisions that affect our society as a whole and have had a tremendous impact on the arts in rural and small communities over the past few years. Because of the strong historical tradition of dualistic thinking in our society, these values collisions consist of what appear to be opposing ideas, representing the polarization that is increasingly prevalent in our society. These include: (1) sacred versus secular, (2) individual versus community, and (3) process versus product. By the very nature of their role in identifying, conserving, celebrating, and transmitting cultural values, the arts are being sucked into the vortex of a complicated and potentially destructive collision between these three opposing value systems.

But, the conflict isn't about the arts, it is about the values some art is expressing. For example, I don't believe the recent NEA controversy and subsequent battle with the evangelical religious right is about pornography, obscenity, and freedom of expression - it is about the inability of people to separate the values the arts represent from the way the arts represent the values. It is a failure to understand what the arts are and what value they have in our society. We are a society that prefers to treat symptoms rather than disease. Consequently, it is easier to kill the messenger than to deal with the message. And, if there is anything the arts do well, to our credit and to everyone's discomfort, it is to speak with a clear and authentic voice about the conditions of the world in which we live. This is why I believe the NEA controversy will never be resolved in the halls of Congress, in the reauthorization of the NEA, or in the courts. This controversy represents a collision between all three of these overarching values and it is not going to go away. The issue isn't pornography or obscenity. The issue isn't public funding for the arts. The issue isn't freedom of expression. The issue is values.

Unfortunately, there is more to this issue than just the arts being under attack from outside our community. I believe many of us involved in the arts are unclear about the values that drive our work and this contributes to an internal values collision that is potentially more damaging than any external attack on the arts. The conflict over the past few years regarding issues surrounding freedom of expression and individual rights versus community standards and responsibility, has been more divisive than most of us are willing to admit. Those of us involved in the arts are also affected by the three overarching values collisions, many times causing us to be in conflict with each other.

Community arts agencies, in particular those that exist in rural and small communities all across this country, are in the greatest jeopardy. The reason is that people in arts organizations in these communities, especially those of us who are arts administrators, are caught in the crossfire between opposing value systems that demand us to choose sides. When this happens in a small community, the results can be devastating. While it is true that the national controversy has not yet found its way into all of our rural and small communities, it is already beginning to happen. All it takes is something small to happen and the entire controversy of art, public funding, pornography, and obscenity rears its ugly head. Most of us who live in and work with these communities are not prepared to address this conflict. Often, those of us in community arts development work find ourselves and our values not only in conflict with those outside the arts community, but also within the arts community, with the very individuals, organizations, and communities with which we work. This is the ethical dilemma we deal with every day and it has taken a tremendous toll on us. It all points to an internal values collision many of us, and the organizations and communities we serve, may not survive. This is the real crisis facing our field. And it is not a crisis we can continue to pretend doesn't exist.

The irony of this is, the arts may be one of the few means by which these overarching values collisions, and the subsequent social disintegration that occurs because of them, can be avoided. This is because the arts are both an individual expression and an invitation to create and celebrate community. This is because the arts express both the sacred and the secular. And, this is because the arts are clearly involved in both the process and product of creative expression. The arts create an invitation for people with diverse views to meet in one place and begin to identify what they share in common. When things go right, when the arts are successful, they can help transform the values collision into community convergence. But this cannot and will not happen until we begin to communicate effectively about who we are, what we do, and why we do it. We must develop a shared language about the values that drive our work in the arts and we must begin to share this with those with whom we work. We have to stop letting others set our agenda and make claims about us and our work that are not true. We cannot do this until we stop talking about the symptoms, and start addressing the critical issues facing our field and our society. If we can do this, perhaps we can do more than just survive the values collisions. Perhaps we can help stop them from happening.

How the Arts Can Survive the Values Collision

We look around us and see our life's work disintegrating. The infrastructures we have built to support the arts in the community setting are collapsing all around us, casualties of the values collision. This is just beginning and it already has taken a tremendous toll on many of us. This is our great crisis. It is not a religious crisis, it is a spiritual crisis. And, if we don't do anything about it, we will end up allowing the deep voice to be silenced. We have to be clear of the values that drive our work. We have to communicate these values more effectively to those around us. And, we have to find new ways to communicate this with those who have preconceived notions of what art is and why it is bad.

It means we have to reframe, retool, and rethink what we are doing. It means we have to pay attention to our own needs and start taking better care of ourselves. We have to identify the theory and practice that defines our profession and the work of the community arts movement as a field. This takes time and effort. It means we have to read and research and study and question. It means we have to pull out and listen to ourselves and to those around us.

Amateur Art Verses Community Arts

There are people who believe that any art that is done by someone who is not "paid" should be called "amateur" art. The fallacy of this is that people mistakenly think that just because someone gets paid to do art it is professional. Some have referred to this preconceived attitude about art in rural and small communities as "urban chauvinism." More accurately, it is "ruralism" and it exists in people who live outside our rural and small communities, and unfortunately, even with some who live in these communities as well. It is as destructive and divisive as any other "ism" we have in our culture. Ruralism mistakenly believes that it is impossible to have anything that could be regarded as professional quality come from a rural or small community. It confuses the concept of non-paid artists as being amateur artists who produce amateur art. In reality, it is more accurate to differentiate between paid-professional and non-paid professional art. Most of us in community arts don't use the term amateur - it betrays the goal of a high quality process that produces a high quality product. If we are not committed to the concept of producing professional quality art in our communities then we shouldn't be doing the work.

Community arts does not mean amateur art. It may mean non-paid professional art. And the "criteria of excellence" may have to be defined differently than it is in larger, metropolitan centers. But that doesn't mean it isn't excellent. One thing we do know - you can't have excellence in the arts if you don't have the opportunity to do art. The most important critical issue relating to community arts in rural and small communities isn't excellence, it is access. It is giving people the opportunity to participate in and experience the arts on a personal basis. We have to have access before we can seriously address the issue of excellence. The fact is, some of the most professionally produced arts experiences I have seen have been by non-paid community artists. Many of these "citizen artists" have outstanding qualifications in their arts discipline, but they have chosen not to make their living doing it. They do other things and their arts experiences are part of how they contribute back to the community.

Even in the midst of this discussion of the values collision, I would do a great disservice to our field if I didn't point out the incredible work being done in our communities to address these issues. There are wonderful success stories. Stories of how communities used the arts to convene and get people together. Stories of how the arts contributed not just to a conflict in a community, but also to the healing. We need to tell these stories.

This values collision and the resulting conflict isn't going away any time soon. And increasingly, the conflict won't be about federal or state funding for the arts. It won't even be about community funding for the arts. If we don't do something and do it quickly, the issue will be whether or not the arts even have a place in our communities. We have to set our own agenda. We have to quit pointing our fingers at the "enemy". There is no enemy - there are just people like us who are frustrated and angry and struggling to survive. We have to find a way to work toward the same goal: vibrant communities that are self-determining their own future.

The arts have always survived. That may be what we do best - survive. Now, perhaps more than ever, survival skills may be our most important contribution to the communities and organizations we serve. We can show them a way to survive that doesn't force us to engage in a cultural and religious war. We can show them an alternative to intolerance. We can do this only if we understand it is not enough to speak the deep voice. We have to listen as well.

The Broken Circle

We live in a world where it is increasingly difficult to articulate the values that tie us together as a community - bond us as a society. Some believe we have lost our grounding, that we are uprooted, untethered, a society drifting toward dissolution. These people live with fear. Some believe we have lost our values altogether. These people have no hope. One thing is clear; we live in a very difficult time of change and transition that leaves most of us confused and concerned.

We have not lost our values as much as we have we lost touch with them. Throughout the history of this country, we have consistently divorced the arts from our everyday lives. We have made art a noun that is bought and sold to the highest bidder. The problem with this is, the arts have always been one of the key ways that a culture's values are identified, conserved, celebrated, and transmitted. Without the arts integrated into our daily lives, we lose an essential way to tell our story. When the arts are viewed only as a "sign," we lose the voice of the imagination - metaphor. The end result of this is, we forget who we are and our culture begins to "dis-integrate" because we have no center, no connecting point, no tether. This is the great spiritual crisis of our time.

By introducing the arts and promoting them in the community setting, we provide a means for our stories to be shared and celebrated together. Thus, the arts, often accused of being the source of the problem, can be a means of restoring our cultural roots and healing the spiritual brokenness of our time.

As long as there are communities, the arts will survive. As long as the arts survive, there will always be communities. They are as essential to each other as any two things can be. The arts nurture the rural genius and the rural genius nurtures the community. And all of it results in the culture - becoming more and more visible, widening the circle larger and larger. This is the way things work in rural and small communities. It has always been this way. And of all the things around us that are changing, this will always stay the same - the arts will always make the circle whole.

The Circle

We are the people of the broken circle,
poets, prophets, and pioneers
who suffer from the blessing and the curse of blind vision.
We are troubadours of a troubled time,
dreamers who reveal what has always been
but never seen before,
wanderers engaged in the quest for authentic community.

We are the singers who have not forgotten the song or how to sing,
dancers who defy the air and risk the leap,
artists who challenge the chaos and shape perceptions into form,
storytellers who mold muse and meaning into words,
seekers, all of us,
inscape artists in search of the soul.

We are the keepers of the fire,
guardians of the great mystery,
protectors of the lost language.
We are the children of the awe,
stewards of the gifts and the grace,
harnessing the power and the paradox
of grassroots and mountain wings.

We are the remnant who remember the future -
we are the dance that makes the circle whole.
Come, dance with us.

Part II

Community Arts Development

Porches and Parlors

Honoring Our Poets, Prophets, and Pioneers

There are literally millions of people in country communities today whose abilities along various lines have been hidden, simply because they have never had an opportunity to give expression to their talents. In many respects this lack of self-expression has been due to the social conditions existing in the country, the narrow-minded attitude of society toward those who till the soil, and the absence of those forces which seek to arouse the creative instincts and stimulate that imagination and initiative in country people which mean leadership.

Alfred Arvold, *The Little Country Theatre*, 1923

It would be better if art were nameless, and that those of us who write about art in books and the reviews and newspapers, always clacking about art, or Art, or ART, were constrained somehow by good taste or a hickory club either to do art in its appropriate human context, and in doing be it, or keep still. For art suffers more than most activities in being withdrawn from the contexts of living. It is categorized as something special.

Baker Brownell, *The Human Community*, 1950

Modern art activity can provide a new birth and new creative directions of usefulness for such a community. As art activity is developed, the community is recreated. The vital roots of every phase of life are touched. As the community is awakened to its opportunity in the arts, it becomes a laboratory through which the vision of the region is reformulated and extended. And as the small community discovers its role, as the small community generates freshness of aesthetic response across the changing American scene, American art and life are enhanced.

Robert Gard, *Arts in The Small Communities*, 1967

When I go into a community and work with individuals in organizations, especially those that are in trouble, one of the very first things I do is to ask them to name their heroes. Every organization has them. Organizations are a community of people gathered together because of shared values, issues, and concerns. And like communities, organizations need to identify their heroes and honor them. It is an essential part of nurturing the corporate culture of the organization. In doing this, remembering and honoring heroes, organizations are reminded of why it is they came into existence in the first place. It is a way of staying in touch with the founding values of those who created the organization to begin with - the driving, creative force that brought the organization into being. This provides them with an essential tether to their past. It is difficult to address their problems and move forward without this vital connection.

Every community has heroes as well. It is important to remember our heroes - the poets, prophets and pioneers - who led the way to where we are now as a community. We lose track of them and the contribution they made to the development of our community. We forget their successes. And just as important, we forget their struggles, and perhaps even their failures. Remembering what didn't work can be as important as remembering what did.

Remembering our heroes, organizational and community, reminds us we did not get here on our own. Others came before us and their stories are a vital part of re-membering our community. When we forget our stories, we lose a very important part of the cultural connection we need to keep us together.

The community arts development movement also has its heroes. They are unique to us and to the work of community-making through the community arts development process. Each one has made a unique and essential contribution. Combined, they bring us to this point in our history as a movement.

Instead of just talking about historical movements, I wanted to devote this essay to those individuals who made the movements happen. They represent some of our most important heroes in the community arts development movement. It is important to look at the people who have gone before us in order to understand who we are as community makers. It is a long history that is unique to rural and small communities. It is a fascinating list of heroes whose contributions help us understand the values that drive our work today. It is a story of self-improvement and self-education. It is a story of self-determination and rural genius. It is a story of porches and parlors, where people gathered together to share, to learn, to create community. It has always been about porches and parlors.

Josiah Holbrook - The First Parlor

Josiah Holbrook was a farmer. But he wasn't satisfied with the life he had - he wanted more. He wanted culture and he wanted education, and he knew he would have to do it himself or he wouldn't get it. So, in 1826, Holbrook invited some neighbors in Millbury, Massachusetts, into his home to study together. They read books and discussed them. They engaged in conversation with each other about what they read. They gathered in Josiah's parlor to study, search, question, and learn. They were their own teachers. Sometimes in the parlor, sometimes on the front porch - always in the atmosphere of respect for knowledge and the desire for learning. It was the best of what the "academy" was always meant to be. This self-study, self-education, self-improvement approach set a precedent for the way most of the community arts development movement would later evolve.

After a period of time, they ran out of things to read and they decided to invite some of the professors from the nearby educational institutions to join them in the parlor for dinner and conversation. This stimulated their learning environment and they continued their quest for culture for years to come.

Eventually, others began to do what Holbrook and his neighbors were doing. Other groups formed, meeting in parlors and on porches all over the countryside. They read and they gathered together and they had conversations about culture and values and the issues of the day.

This is how it all began. People wanting to improve themselves through self-education. And it spread. Before too long, these different groups got together and decided to organize, forming the American Lyceum Association in 1831. The purpose of the Lyceum was to create an association of adults committed to self-education and the exploration of culture. With the increase in the number of Lyceum groups, the demand for speakers increased. Eventually, this resulted in the "paid honorarium," making it possible for sought-after speakers to make their living on the

Lyceum Association circuit. By 1850, it is estimated that there were over 3,000 Lyceums in existence in communities of every size across the country (Case, 1948). All of this happened in just over twenty years.

Before I move on, there are three things on which I want to focus. The first is the fact that this effort was self-initiated. Most significant historical events affecting rural and small communities in this country were self-initiated, either by an individual or group of individuals.

The second is that the desire for self-improvement usually involves other people. Education is about more than knowing information, it is about the knowledge of what to do with the information we have acquired. The application of knowledge into the affairs and conduct of the human community is an important element of what it means to be educated.

The third observation is the fact that once the "paid honorarium" was introduced, the Lyceum Movement changed. This represents the first of many times when programs initiated to meet rural needs for self-improvement and self-education were transformed into commodity-based, profit-making experiences. Throughout the history of the community arts development movement, we will see this time and time again.

What we have failed to remember is Josiah Holbrook's vision and the fact his effort was successful because it was a small group of people gathered together. It took place in the environment of someone's home, meeting in the parlor or on the front porch. When it moved from the parlor and front porch, it lost part of the reason for its success. It lost touch with the unique values of rural and small community life that created it.

In 1867, James Redpath took the paid honorarium concept one step further by creating the Redpath Lyceum Bureau. His Bureau would become the general headquarters and chief booking office for the lucrative Lyceum lecture circuit. The speakers bureau revolutionized the Lyceum movement by streamlining the booking process and making the most efficient use of time and talent of the speakers. He put Lyceum speakers on a speaking circuit, sending them out in an ordered, planned, organized system making their lives and their travels easier. It also made it easier for the lecturers to get to those cities that were located on the rail. Those outside the area served by the railroad were left out of the circuit. As the speaker's bureau concept grew, most of the local self-improvement clubs began to disappear. It was the first of many local community, self-improvement efforts that were eventually transformed into profit-making ventures that benefited a few people, a lot.

Dr. John Heyl Vincent - The Chautauqua

How can we get teachers to teach better? That was the question our second hero, a minister, asked himself. His name was John Heyl Vincent, and in 1874 he started a Methodist summer Sunday School camp at Chautauqua Lake in rural western New York. Dr. Vincent believed strongly in the role of arts and culture in the teaching and learning process. The name Chautauqua soon became synonymous with the word culture. One of the reasons for its success was Dr. Vincent included the arts in his Sunday School camp experience in order to help people study the Bible. He knew something then that we are just now beginning to understand - the arts aren't just a subject to teach. The arts are also a wonderful way to teach other subjects. It was a new way to approach teacher training.

Teachers were introduced to the arts as a way of teaching the lessons of the Bible. They were also given the opportunity to participate in the arts during the camp experience. They participated in the arts themselves and experienced the arts as audience members. The Chautauqua was a total cultural environment and its reputation grew. Whether it was the subject matter, the location, or the timing, no one is sure. But the result was it eventually became one of this country's most vigorous private movements in popular education (Gould, 1961).

Chautauqua rapidly impacted rural communities through the development of the Chautauqua Literary and Scientific Circles. Dr. Vincent believed that there needed to be resources to assist individuals in their study of the biblical and cultural traditions that had become so much a part of the Chautauqua experience. In 1878, he decided to expand the Chautauqua movement by announcing plans for the formation of a study-group format and embarked on a four-year program of guided reading. As these resources were developed, he decided it should be shared with others around the country who might not be able to attend the New York Chautauqua. The material was printed and sent out on a regular basis as lesson material that could be studied by the

Literary and Scientific Circles. Once again, people gathered in parlors and on front porches in rural and small communities, using the Chautauqua study material as a resource for self-education. The success of this small study-group format was that it was with people who knew each other, who gathered together to talk and learn from each other. The Literary Circles were a huge success.

It is estimated by 1878, that over 84,000 persons, mostly from the Midwest, had joined these self-improvement circles and continued the tradition of art and culture in rural communities as a process of self-education and self-improvement (Gould, 1961). Once again we see the influence of the small gatherings of people engaged in conversation with each other about the arts and culture of their day. It was the basis for discovery, and it was fun. The Chautauqua Literary and Scientific Circles became part of the community-making tradition of the day. The success of the Circles also brought about an increased interest to "recreate" the New York Chautauqua experience, establishing what were called "Independent Chautauquas." These were efforts to replicate the original Chautauqua experience in other communities. Most of the independent Chautauquas developed in the larger cities and this further spread the influence of the New York Chautauqua.

The Chautauqua was about people learning by talking and listening to each other. The arts were a vital part of this experience, playing a key role in the educational process. The arts were not the main emphasis, but rather helped express what was important to the people participating in the Camp. People gathered together, studied, talked, and learned, following the front porch and parlor tradition of Josiah Holbrook. This was not the first marriage between art and institutional religion in the United States, but it is certainly one of the most successful. Dr. Vincent was not promoting art, he was promoting art as a way to learn and a way to teach. Dr. Vincent is a hero because he was innovative. He is also a hero because he risked bringing something new into existence. The relationship between the church and the arts had always been an uneasy alliance. He ventured forth into new territory and, unknown to him, advanced the role of the arts more than anyone else in his day. We know very little about the man, but we know a great deal about his work and the impact it had on community-making. This is usually the case with people who are unsung heroes.

Keith Vawter - The Tent Chautauqua

Our third hero is Keith Vawter. Like James Redpath, Vawter saw a need and created something to fill the void. In 1902, he became the manager of the Redpath Chicago Lyceum Speakers Bureau. Vawter recognized that the Independent Chautauqua experience could be enhanced by better planning and use of more speakers. This, coupled with the fact he had Lyceum Speakers who were available to him in the summer, gave him the idea of combining the two together. Vawter combined the Lyceum Speakers Bureau with the Chautauqua traveling shows. In addition, he knew that most rural communities did not have the facilities to accommodate the Independent Chautauqua experience.

To remedy this, and increase his potential market, Vawter purchased a used circus tent that could provide a portable meeting place for the programs. The tent symbolized the combined adventure of the circus with the tradition of the religious revival and helped break through what had, for many years, been a difficult audience to reach. It became, in a sense, a portable front porch to which he could invite the entire community.

Vawter played on the indirect certification of the original Chautauqua because it started as a Methodist church training experience. This led people to believe it was supported by the Church, even though the Tent Chautauqua had no connection whatsoever to the original Sunday School camp experience. The Tent Chautauqua Circuit reached its peak in 1924, with the Jubilee Year Celebration of the original Chautauqua. This celebration involved over 12,000 towns, reaching a rural and small community audience estimated to be over 35 million people (Case, 1948). Following the Jubilee Year, the Tent Chautauqua Circuit ceased to exist.

The Tent Chautauqua increased the opportunities for people in rural communities to experience the arts and culture on a personal basis by being members of an audience. In addition, it greatly expanded rural people's oneness to theatre, overcoming an intense prejudice and animosity that had existed for years. To many people in rural and small communities, theatre was considered evil (Case, 1948). Gradually, over the years, theatre experiences were introduced in the Tent Chautauqua programs. First in readings and monologues and then in cuttings from plays. The impact this had was enormous as it coincided with the development of theatre as a course of study in colleges and universities. It also coincided with the development of the Little Theatre Movement (also known as the Community Theatre Movement). These three elements, The Tent Chautauqua, theatre in colleges and universities, and the Little Theatre Movement, dramatically changed the way communities understood and supported the arts.

Our first three heroes, Josiah Holbrook, Dr. Heyl Vincent, and Keith Vawter, all added considerably to understanding the role of the arts in the community-making process. They were clearly heroes of the community arts development movement. Without question, they were pioneers, bringing into existence a whole new understanding of the role of art in the lives of those who lived in rural and small communities.

George Pierce Baker - Development of Educational Theatre

Most Puritan-related schools and colleges were marked by the same antagonism toward the theatre which was prevalent in the rural community setting. This antagonism lasted well into the nineteenth century. At the turn of the twentieth century, theatre became a more acceptable form of extracurricular participatory experience for college students. In 1905, George Pierce Baker was able to help bring about a change in attitude toward theatre. Although he was not the first to introduce dramatic (stage) technique into the college curriculum, his classes became some of the most well-known theatre courses offered (Wallace, 1954). In 1905, he introduced English 47 at Harvard, a course in play writing for graduate students. He moved to Yale in 1925, where he was given direction of the new graduate school of drama, complete with a playhouse and curriculum in theatre arts.

Baker's contribution to educational theatre was enormous and it extended beyond just the educational institution. Because of Baker and others at the turn of the century, students were able to experience theatre on a personal basis by doing theatre, not just reading it. They read plays and then they acted, giving life to the stories and the characters. As they left Harvard, Yale, and the other colleges and universities, they wanted more. The fact these courses coincided with the development of the Little Theatre Movement is probably no coincidence at all. In fact, Baker is often credited with stimulating the Little Theatre Movement, then in its infancy. This interest and development in the area of theatre at the college and university level continued to develop. It eventually contributed to the growth of independent "speech and dramatic arts" departments in colleges and universities all across the United States (Wallace, 1954).

Percey MacKaye - The Community Theatre Movement

The community theatre movement took hold at the turn of the century. The impetus for the movement was the dissatisfaction with the "for-profit" Broadway theatre. One of the first major proponents of this movement was Percy MacKaye. MacKaye believed the importance of the opportunity to do Civic Theatre was that it provided people the opportunity to participate in theatre, not just watch it. MacKaye wanted to take the theatre experience out of the hands of the "merchants of art" by elimination of private profit and establishing public support for theatre (MacKaye, 1912). He believed this provided a service to the entire community. This is the first of many associations made between community theater and service.

While the title Civic Theatre did not take hold, the concept did. This new way of looking at theatre in rural areas and small communities began the shift away from art being understood as something people supported and enjoyed as an audience, to that in which they could participate themselves. The primary focus was on self-improvement and the personal experience individuals had in the arts.

His contribution was expanded in 1917, when Louise Burleigh used the term Community Theatre. This term did stick. Many of these new community theatre organizations were located in the larger cities, and broke the bond of Broadway. A major contribution of the community theatre movement was to bring the theatre experience to many rural areas and small communities all across America. One of the catalysts for this was the establishment of the Drama League in Evanston, Illinois. Formed in 1910, its main goal was to bring better plays to small towns. The original purpose of the League was to build up audiences for theatre through study courses, reading circles, and lectures and to help audiences develop their appreciation for dramatic literature (Wilson, 1982). Hundreds of these study groups were formed throughout the country, repeating the earlier front porch and parlor study groups of the Lyceum and Chautauqua experiences.

One of the values driving the work of MacKaye, and eventually the Drama League, was the fact they considered the theatre a natural part of the expansion of ideas which ultimately brought tolerance and understanding to all citizens in the community. The Drama League recognized the unique opportunity furnished by Little Theatres and Community Theatres to provide these experiences to remote communities cut off from professional attractions. They outlined a plan for establishing community threatre groups around each state.

The efforts of the Drama League, combined with the work of MacKaye, Burleigh, Harold Pierce Baker, and others, helped theatre in the community setting take hold as a strong movement in the United States. It has been estimated there were over 141,000 community theatre groups in America by the 1950's. A more conservative estimate was that there were over 3,500 full-scale community theatres in the United States on a continuing basis (Gard & Burley, 1959).

Adelia Cone, J. Milnor Dorey, and Alice Minie Herts

It is nearly impossible to single out only a few high school teachers who can be called heroes. But, there are three at the beginning of the twentieth century, who stand out because of their early contribution to understanding theatre as a way of inspiring students to greater learning.

Adelia Cone believed there were educational potentialities inherent in dramatic activity that went beyond teaching students to act on a stage. She approached drama from a holistic point of view understanding that it taught co-operation and discipline and inspired students to greater learning (Cone, 1912).

J. Milnor Dorey believed it was the duty of schools not only to train the mind but also to develop forceful students with attractive personalities. He believed high school dramatics could do this by developing three qualities. The first was resourcefulness acquired by students memorizing a part for a play. The second was gaining knowledge of human nature by portraying various roles and learning what makes people act the way they do. The third was the sense of community that comes out of the team-work involved in putting on a play (Wallace, 1982).

Alice Minie Herts founded the Educational Theatre for Children and Young People in New York. She believed that dramatic instinct was too often confused with dramatic talent. She believed that participation in drama brought about a cultivation of the imagination and, as a result, brought something into existence which did not previously exist for the child (Wallace, 1982).

All three of these teachers, as well as countless thousands of others, knew drama provided a wonderful learning environment. They knew that as children did art, they learned much more. This commitment, combined with the growth of the influence of the Tent Chautauqua and the Little Theatre Movement, created a whole new understanding of the role of drama. Suddenly, drama was not just story telling - it had become part of the story-making process, contributing to the lives of those who participate in the experience of telling someone else's story. It is hard to imagine the impact these teachers had on the lives of their students. We know this tradition continues today. It is not in all schools and it is not in all drama programs. But there are still the Adelia Cones, Milnor Doreys, and Alice Minie Herts out there, reaching out to young people, inviting them into the circle on stage, changing their lives.

Alfred Arvold - The Little Country Theatre

In the 1920's, a man by the name of Alfred G. Arvold, combined the efforts of educational and community theatre. Educated at the University of Wisconsin at Madison, he taught high school in several Wisconsin communities before moving to North Dakota. He then became a faculty member for the Agricultural College of North Dakota State University. Arvold believed that social stagnancy was a characteristic trait of the small town and country community. He also believed it did not have to be this way. Arvold believed that most people never realized their full abilities because they had never been given the opportunity to express their talents. Given the invitation and the opportunity to participate in this expression, he believed country people could discover their creative instincts. He also believed nurturing the creative instincts in people directly impacted their imagination and initiative, translating into leadership. This is one of the first instances in the community arts development movement where the arts and leader-development are directly linked.

Arvold traveled the North Dakota landscape, working with people in rural, isolated communities, to tap into this new leadership resource. He believed that it was a natural condition for people to crave self-expression and that community theatre, or "Country Theatre," as he called it, could satisfy this need and be a force to democratize art so that the average citizen could appreciate it (Arvold, 1923). Arvold recognized that efforts to build a community must come from within and he believed that community theatre could provide the creative stimulation and catalyst for this community building effort to occur. He did this by helping them to present plays. He also accomplished this by encouraging people in these country communities to write their own stories and produce them on stage. Arvold's work is among the first that uses the arts to fulfill the mandate of the Smith-Lever act (1914), requiring land-grant universities to serve the communities. Without question, this man was a pioneer. His work is among the first work that can be clearly defined as community arts development.

The development of the community theatre movement represents an important part of the development of arts in rural and small communities. It combined the "self-improvement" and "self-education" concept of the original Lyceum and Chautauqua experiences with opportunities to participate in the arts experience on a personal basis. It took art out of the realm of the passive into the new arena of active participation and personal experience and creating that opportunity for persons in most rural communities. Thanks to the work in community theatre of Arvold, and others who followed, people in rural and small communities discovered the transforming power of art in their own lives. They discovered they didn't have to tell someone else's story, they had their own story to tell.

Arvold's work opened the door to a new understanding of the role of art in rural and small communities. It also set in motion the contemporary manifestation of the community arts movement. The work of Arvold was pioneering. It was also prophetic as it led the way for what was to come - a growing realization that the gifts of creative ability are every bit as present and powerful in rural and small communities as they are anywhere else. He was among the first to recognize the gift of rural genius and develop a program to identify it and help people in these small communities and country places do something to celebrate it. He was also among the first to use theatre to nurture this important natural resource that resulted in leadership.

Baker Brownell - The Montana Project

One of the earliest community development projects to use the arts was the Montana Project, and it took place in the 1940's. This project was directed by Baker Brownell, one of the pioneers in the community development movement. He used the arts as a way of helping people in Anaconda, Montana, tell their story and get in touch with what was going on with their community following the closing of the Anaconda Copper Mine.

Brownell is probably the central figure responsible for writing down the early philosophical tradition that underpins our work in community arts. His books *Art is Action* and *The Human Community* are essential reading for anyone interested in the community arts development process.

Brownell believed the real problem with art is that it is continually taken out of the context in which it is created. From his perspective, this transforms the art from expression to object and, when this happens, it loses its real value. Baker Brownell understood the vital role the arts play in the total community setting. This understanding, combined with his writing and his field practice, provides us with an invaluable resource for helping us identify the theory and practice of the community arts field.

Brownell is truly one of the great unsung heroes of the community arts development movement. We need to reacquaint ourselves with his writing. But, as valuable as his writing is, it is his work as a practitioner where we can discover the real wealth of his contribution to our field.

Robert Gard - The Windmill Man

I cannot think of a single human being in our country who has made a more lasting and significant impact on the community arts movement than Robert Gard. Founder of the Wisconsin Idea Theatre, Gard created an extension outreach program in the College of Agriculture at the University of Wisconsin. His commitment was to training rural playwrights as a form of creating and sustaining a "true regional theatre." He believed that theatre was the traditional nursery of all the arts and provided the invitation for people to produce the best and the greatest that their energy, strength, knowledge, and sense of beauty can produce (Gard & Burley, 1959).

One of the most important contributions Gard made was the realization that individuals were the real storytellers. Consequently, he spent the majority of his life encouraging people to write their stories and produce them as plays. This was how he believed the arts could make a direct contribution to the development of individuals and the communities in which they lived.

Gard directed a program that was the first project funded by the newly formed National Endowment for the Arts program, designed to develop the arts in rural communities. In 1967, he worked with five rural communities in Wisconsin to start arts councils. The project report was published under the name, *The Arts, A National Plan* (now known as the Windmill Book), and was designed to encourage the development of community arts councils all across America.

There is probably no one who has contributed more to the community arts development movement than Robert Gard. His pioneering work continues to show how the arts, when translated into the daily lives of people, can alter the face of America.

Summary

As one examines the contribution of these heroes and the historical movements they started, at least four patterns emerge. The first is a pattern of creativeness and innovation at the community level that translates into new ways to meet community needs. It is an approach to art and culture as a process of self-improvement, self-expression, and self-education. This pattern represents the value of art as a process to be participated in and experienced on a personal basis. This is an essential core value of the community arts development process.

A second pattern that emerges is that of individuals outside rural communities who took early efforts at self-improvement and self-expression, and turned them into money making ventures that changed the value of art from process and participation to that of commodity or product. Frequently, what started out as celebration of self-expression and self-education, quickly became entrepreneurial, profit-making ventures. These marketplace schemes contradicted the original values that brought the self-expression and self-education experience into existence. The "merchants of art" who promote art as a product to be bought and sold have always found rural communities an excellent resource and an excellent marketplace.

A third pattern emerged through the efforts of people like Alfred Arvold and Robert Gard, representing a value orientation based on art and culture as both process and product, keeping the arts centered in the community and central to the life of the people who lived there. This tradition continues today with those working in the arts who understand that bringing art into the community needs to be balanced with efforts to nurture the arts within the community. It is this core value system upon which the philosophical foundation of the community arts development movement and our work as professionals is based.

A final pattern to note is the continuing uneasy and tenuous relationship between the arts and the church. The early Puritan-influenced value system viewed the arts as potential expression of evil and wickedness that was a threat to the piety of the individual. While the Chautauqua provided an alternative view of art, it did not fully overcome these early prejudices. We see the result of this unresolved conflict in the controversy over public funding for the arts that has dominated the decade of the 1990's. This uneasy alliance between art and religion continues to be one of the major barriers to advancing the role of the arts in rural and small communities.

There is ample evidence to support the conclusion that the arts in rural communities have enriched the cultural development of the arts in all communities, large and small. This is because the community arts development movement has always understood that along with the cultural treasures brought into the community, there are cultural treasures created within the community, and these need to be nurtured and valued as well. This dual focus on process and product continues to be the guiding force behind the development of the arts in rural and small communities all across the United States.

We work in an important field. We have a long history and tradition. We also have powerful heroes whose vision and determination continues to influence our work of rebuilding of the front porch of America.

The history of the community arts development movement in rural and small communities is a long, rich heritage of innovative individuals, philosophical traditions, and creative community efforts, whose existence continues to change the inscape of

America's rural and small communities. Each region has its own unique history and heroes that need to be identified and celebrated. Each community has its own cultural roots that need to be remembered, restored, and honored. Each organization has its own heroes as well. We need to identify these individuals and celebrate their contributions. When we do this, we reconnect ourselves to our own story, reminding us of why we do the work we do. We might also feel a little less alone and isolated in our work, knowing there is a whole host of poets, prophets, and pioneers who have forged the trail for us.

The Art of Community-Making

Community Arts Development in Action

While casting for a musical production I was directing for the Boonville Community Theatre, I had two people audition for the same role - one was the publisher of the community newspaper and the other was the custodian at the same newspaper. They were both qualified for the role and I knew both could handle the character. I ended up casting the custodian in the role, fully conscious of the potential conflict this might create for me and the two individuals involved. What happened was not what I expected. The publisher accepted a position in the chorus and during the rehearsals, he and the custodian spent time together, getting to know each other (as only backstage conversation can do). Suddenly, the artificial distinction of position between them disappeared. They were just two people working together to help put on a musical production. It was one of the surprises and one of the joys of my experience in community theatre.

A good community theatre production takes everyone working together to make it happen. As we work together through all of the rehearsals, set-building, and all the various aspects of putting on a theatrical production, we are engaged in the community arts development process. Being with each other, dealing with stress and tension, and working together toward a common goal is part of community-making. When we put on a performance we invite people from the larger community to gather together, share a common experience, and celebrate the gifts of who we are as a people. This is the way it is for all community arts experiences. It doesn't always work the way we want it to, but community-making should always be a goal of the community arts experience.

Who We Are as Community Makers

Language has always been a problem for our field. Are we administrators, managers, directors, or supervisors? Are the organizations with which we work community organizations, community arts organizations, community arts councils, community arts agencies, local arts agencies, or cultural institutions? Are we engaged in community development, community arts development, or community cultural development? While all of these are related terms, each one has a different meaning to different people. Each one also requires very specific skills related to the unique context in which the work exists. We have historically failed to recognize these differences and, in the process, failed to define the field in which we work. One reason for this may be that the work and the field in which we work are relatively new. Another may be the fact that so many of us are "cross-discipliners," coming from many different professions. In addition, many of us are double-dominants, strong in both artistic and administrative ability. Another significant contributing factor may be the fact there is no single career preparation route one takes to enter the field of community arts development. In fact, many of us had no formal education and/or training for the entry-level positions in which we started. This has always been primarily a practice-oriented field. At least, it has been so up to now. The question is - to what profession do we belong? Is there a term that defines the work we do? Does it matter? Yes, it does. And working to find shared definitions and create a shared language should be one of the challenges we address together.

Community-Making

From the earliest efforts of organized community development, the arts have been an important part in the effort to help individuals in communities of all sizes grow and develop. In the process, the arts have also played an essential role in helping a community celebrate who it is as a collection of individuals who make up the larger community. Eventually these early community development efforts, (started in the first part of this century with work in community theatre), came to be known as community arts development. In recent years , this term is increasingly being used interchangeably with the term, community cultural development. Community cultural development does the same thing as community arts development except it broadens its efforts to include all cultural organizations in the community (libraries, historical societies, museums, schools, etc.). Its focus is somewhat broader as well, addressing the larger contribution the arts make to the identify, conserve, celebrate, and transmit core cultural values of the community, in particular, values of diversity. In essence, they both do the same thing in different ways. They both understand the important role the arts play in the daily lives of individuals and the communities in which they live. While the term community cultural development is a useful distinction, for the purpose of this book, the focus will be on the community arts development process.

The term community arts development points to the unique aspect of our work in the arts. There are several additional words that connect all of these approaches into what we could call the field of community arts development. The most important word is community. This is the essential defining word describing the context in which we do our work. The second word that clarifies what it is we do in this particular context of community is "making" - we are about "community-making." This term goes beyond the traditional community arts development term, focusing on more than those things specifically connected to the arts, and encompasses all of the various subcategories I have listed in this essay. It also goes beyond the more frequently used term "community arts development," pointing to the role the arts play in the broader community setting without getting confused with the word culture (many people see no difference between the words art and culture). One thing the term community-making has over the other terms, is the fact it makes reference to the power of the creative act itself. This brings into focus the fact that what we do is involved in the creative act of "making" something that didn't previously exist - in this context, community. This is why the term community-making points to the heart and soul of what it is we do through the community arts development process and defines what it is we are doing when we engage in this work.

The Context - Where We Do Community-Making

Now that we have discussed who we are, we need to tackle where it is we do what we do. That is, in what context do we work as community makers? Since this book's primary focus is on community arts development in rural and small communities, it is important to establish a working definition of the terms "rural," "small," and "community."

The word "rural" means different things to people. It covers a large continuum of geographic locations, population density, and community-making structures. For some, it is a positive word, conjuring up scenes of pastoral harmony and idyllic existence ("the way things used to be"). For others, it is a negative word that implies an unsophisticated, uneducated, and undeveloped back-roads existence. It's not that the word "rural" is bad. But it is a word that frequently conjures up images that are not always accurate and are many times limiting. The term "rural" isn't inclusive enough to be useful on its own, especially as it relates to the community arts development process. This is where the addition of the word "small" adds clarification. When used in conjunction with "rural," the word "small" provides a more inclusive picture of the communities we serve. In this context, the word small is generally, but not always, used to identify those communities with populations of less than 50,000 (SMSA governmental population designation for "city"). Sometimes we refer to these as "micropolitans." Many times we just call them small cities. They can also be suburban areas, connected to the larger metropolitan areas by being linked to the outer rim of a large population center.

This is not to say you cannot have a small community in a larger metropolitan setting. There are a lot of community arts development experiences that are successful in this larger setting. But almost all of them are designated for a particular aspect of the population, some defined community group such as a neighborhood, youth center, parks program, school program, etc. Therefore, the term rural and small community is generally used to designate a broad host of communities existing outside the larger metropolitan, urban centers of our nation. And there are a lot of these communities in existence in the United States.

The advantage of using the term small is that it doesn't provide a simple, clear-cut, meaning that limits the definition. The use of both terms, rural and small together, is a more complete and inclusive way to define the context in which we do our work. It doesn't have the negative connotations of using just rural, but it also provides a broader and more clear definition of the constituency being served.

This brings us to our third and final word needing definition, "community." This one is not as easy to define. A colleague recently asked me to define what I meant by the term "community." I responded somewhat reluctantly that the term community was too difficult to narrow to only one definition. I then quickly added, "But I know it when I feel it." From this perspective, community is much more a "state of being" than a "place of residence."

What we do know is the concept of community is not limited to geography or population density. It is almost impossible to find a rural or small community that is still totally geographically isolated. Because of this, increasingly, community is defined less by geographical location and more by shared values, interests, and concerns. These are the things that bring people together. These are also the things that keep people together. These are the relationships that make community what it is. With this definition, it is entirely possible to live in one particular geographic location and not "be part of a community." In fact, this is increasingly becoming the case. This is why rural and small communities are at risk.

The 1989 *Webster's Encyclopedic Unabridged Dictionary of the English Language* gives us two different, distinctive meanings of the word. First, *A social group of any size whose members reside in a specific locality, share government, and have a common cultural and historical heritage.* The second, *A social group sharing common characteristics or interests and perceived or perceiving itself as distinct in some respect from the larger society within which it exists.* These two definitions identify two types of communities we serve in community arts development. The specific community of those individuals and collections of individuals involved in the arts, and the larger, geographic locality in which we live.

The word community comes from the Latin word *communi(s)* and it means "in common or to be as one." Our word communication shares the same root. Thus, it is fair to say, one working definition that might be appropriate is that community is what happens when people communicate with each other. But it isn't just communication that matters. It is the kind of communication. It is a communication that implies both talking and listening. It is a communication that is based on the participants being equal, regardless of their social, economic, or religious status. It is a communication that suggests an interdependence, things shared in common; in particular, values. All of these combine to form an emotional and spiritual bond that ties us together in relationship with each other. This is community.

The phrase rural and small community is a positive and inclusive way to identify the context in which we do our community arts development work. It shifts the focus from geography and population density to that of a group of people with common values, interests, and concerns. Thus, the essential word is not rural or small, but community. For those of us who work in this context, this is the word that more accurately communicates the work we do. Not only is the context different in rural and small communities, so is the community arts development process within this context. That is, how we go about doing what it is we do. Being clear about identifying the context in which we do our work will help us identify the resources needed to get the work done.

What Community Arts Development Is
And How We Do It

Now that we have a clearer idea of who we are and where it is we do our community-making work, we need to discuss what it is we do as community makers and how we go about doing it. This requires another set of definitions. We have traditionally referred to this work as community arts development. That is, we are community makers who use the community arts development process to make community. The process we use is based on the core value that art is "for the doing" and for "learning through the doing." Community arts development is the process through which we invite individuals to experience on a personal basis. In community arts development, individuals are not observers, they are participants. It is not just about bringing art from outside the community for people to see and enjoy. It is also about bringing out the art that is in the community, inside the people who make the community what it is. This is not to take away from the performances/product aspect of art. This also plays an important role in the community arts development process. But the final product/performance is not the primary focus. Community arts development is based on a balance between the process and the product. The goal is not only to produce a program or performance, but also to provide a positive process in which individuals participate in the arts. My first experience with community arts was based on this notion of balance.

In 1978, a group of citizens responded to an ad in the local newspaper for anyone interested in producing a community musical. We met in Thespian Hall. It was so cold in the theater you could see the words of each person as they spoke (it was winter and we couldn't afford to have the heat on in the theater). It was that evening a group of citizens in Boonville, Missouri, committed themselves to putting on a musical. This was a monumental effort. There was no organized community theatre group, no money, and little experience. And there was no community arts program in place to support it. This experience would be the catalyst for the creation of such a program. Once we decided to do the show, I made a few closing comments as the person who would direct the show. I told the thirty-plus people there that I didn't care what happened on July 6, 7, and 8 (our production dates). What I was more concerned about was what happened between then (February 22nd) and the actual performances. If we worked together, learned together, and took risks together, whatever we did as a performance would reflect this. It worked. And it worked well. It worked because we were all intentional about what it was we were doing. It worked because we all took the risk together. And it worked because we had fun doing it. Not all community theatre experiences I have been involved in were as successful as this first one. But the ones that were successful, were successful because they paid attention as much to the process as to the product.

Community-Making and Community Arts Development

Community arts development has three main areas of focus - the individual, the community of arts, and the larger community in which they both exist. First, let's look at the role of the arts as it relates to the individual. The primary focus is first and foremost on the individual. This is the "intra personal" benefit that can result from individuals participating in the community arts experience. Community arts focus on encouraging, developing, and celebrating the unique gifts and creative abilities of all individuals. Community arts development theory believes that as the individuals' gifts and abilities are nurtured, so is their sense of who they are, developing them as individuals and helping them be self-asserting leaders. It is this experience in the arts that involves individuals in self-expression and creative risk-taking, both of which can have a tremendous transforming impact on the individual. It is the continuation of the long tradition of "porches and parlors," the roles of self-education, self-improvement, and self-expression.

The second kind of community-making we do through the community arts development process is to focus on creating the positive environment in which these individual experiences in the arts can be shared. We focus on creating organizations that consist of the individuals involved in the arts and the work they do together as artists. Community arts development creates and nurtures strong community arts agencies, focusing on organizational development issues relating to volunteer and staff leadership, organizational communications and design, and resource development and funding, to name a few. Thus, as we provide these experiences for individual creative expression, we are involved in the very unique work of making, nurturing, and building a "community of arts." This recognizes the fact that a community arts agency/organization is a community of individuals who have values, interests, and concerns in common. It also recognizes that the strength and vitality of this "organizational community" is vital to the quality of the opportunities they offer to individuals to be together with others who share the same interests, values, and concerns.

The third focus is the larger community served by the community arts experience. This contribution of community arts underscores the unique role the arts play in identifying, conserving, celebrating, and transmitting the core, cultural values of a community. As the arts are shared, an "interpersonal" benefit is received from both the audience and those sharing the art. This is the larger "community-making" aspect of community arts development. This is when the community arts experience provides a gathering place for the larger community to gather together to share an experience in common with each other. This is when the community arts experience has its largest impact by helping people of diverse backgrounds gather together and celebrate who they are as a community - who they are "in common." I know very few things that provide this type of diverse gathering place. The arts provide an opportunity to put a name to what is happening around them, inviting the whole community to share, discuss, and respond. As an invitation to community conversation, this is community arts development at its "community-making" best.

When the community arts development process works, all three of these foci come together. The individual, the community of arts, and the community as a whole. They are connected by the vitality and excitement of the arts experience. Participant and audience alike are affected by the process and the product. By working in this very unique and specialized community arts development process, individuals are helped to discover their own creativeness, unleashing creative potential that can, and often does, affect other facets of their lives. Organizations are strengthened and are better able to nurture the individual and the community of arts as a whole. The larger community of individuals is also affected as it is provided with a gathering place, a front porch of sorts, on which everyone can be together, celebrating who they are as a community.

The Community Arts Development Process
in Rural and Small Communities

Now that we have addressed shared language and terminology, I want to move to something else that needs to be understood. Community-making and the community arts development process in the rural and small community context is different. This sounds simple and straight forward enough to go without saying. But if that were so, I wouldn't be addressing this issue. The fact is, there are a lot of people who do not understand there is a difference, and as a result, do not understand community-making in the rural and small community context. Not only is community-making in rural and small communities different, so is the way in which we go about doing this work. In many rural and small communities, there are no paid professional arts administrators. But it is important to note there have always been community makers. One of the sources of community-making that has emerged during the past twenty-five years is the organizational system called the community arts agency. A broadly defined, multi-discipline, community-based organization that is usually nonprofit, tax-exempt, and staffed by volunteers, or part-time, or first-position, full-time arts administrators.

The Friends of Historic Boonville definitely fit this profile. In 1975, the Friends unexpectedly found themselves in the community arts business because someone purchased and donated Thespian Hall to the organization. This was not part of their plan as a historic preservation group, but it was consistent with their mission, since Thespian Hall was the oldest theater in continuous use west of the Allegheny Mountains (built in 1854). They suddenly found themselves owners and landlord of a facility. It changed the organization forever.

After renovating the theater and putting on their first arts festival in the summer of 1976, I was hired by the Friends of Historic Boonville to run Thespian Hall. What they hired me to do was to manage the theater and develop some programming for it. I was a facilities manager. What I ended up doing, not necessarily knowing or understanding this was what I was doing, was community arts development. The city of Boonville had a wonderful performance facility and no organized arts organizations/arts programs to take advantage of it (this is usually opposite of what exists in most communities). I instinctively knew this would not change until we helped create a "felt need" in the community. This happened dramatically during the next eight years. In the beginning, the Friends provided all of the community arts programming that took place in the community. Eventually, we helped to create and support single discipline, non-profit, arts organizations including a community theatre, community band, community chorus, and an incorporated visual art league. While still the major provider of arts experiences, the Friends have now formed strategic partnerships with these organizations and work together with them to provide the community arts experiences for Boonville. This story is not uncommon in rural and small communities.

As shown by this one story, most community arts agencies don't fit the traditional arts council structure. In many communities they may even be the sole provider of arts programs and experiences available to the citizens in a community. One of the things we do know is that few community arts agencies in rural and small communities provide technical assistance for other arts organizations. They are usually organizations that require technical assistance themselves. In some communities, the agencies may be the only arts organization in existence, being the main provider of community arts programming experiences. Few of these agencies have paid staff, and those who do are often unable to pay well enough to get and/or keep trained community arts administrators in that position. Often they can only afford part-time administrators; most of whom have had little or no prior training to taking this position. This is one of the major problems facing organizations in rural and small communities.

Community arts development focuses on encouraging, developing, and celebrating the unique gifts and creative abilities of individuals. In this process, the arts are not viewed as a product, a performance, or an event, that citizens attend or support. They are viewed as a process, providing an opportunity for citizens to participate in and experience them on a personal basis. What this does is to invite individuals to discover who they are, what they believe, and why they believe it. It provides an opportunity for "lifelong learning" that can result in individual change and transformation. This is when the "art we do" is less important than the values that drive us to "do our art." This doesn't reduce the importance of the arts product/ performance or the importance of the quality of those products, whether they are imported from outside the community or produced by the community itself. It just recognizes that the quality of the process will have a direct impact on the quality of the product. By working in this very unique and specialized community arts development process, individuals are helped to discover their own creativeness, unleashing creative potential that can and often does, affect other facets of their lives. The key word here is participation. And where participation occurs, individual ownership is developed. This gives individuals the opportunity to participate in the creative process of self-discovery, while at the same time, working together to develop a new configuration of community organization.

What we have learned through years of efforts is that solutions and structures cannot be superimposed on rural and small communities from the outside and be expected to work. Whatever is done in this setting must be owned by those who live in the community itself. It must be a part of their lives, fitting in and being integrated within their systems and social infrastructure. This is why being a community arts administrator in this context should be viewed as an area of specialization requiring generalist skills. It requires important communication and community organizing skills that challenge the tradition of this being viewed as an "entry level" position for arts administrators. Work in rural and small communities is not something everyone is prepared or trained to do. This is especially the case when it comes to the community arts experience. We need to recognize this and develop new strategies to provide professional development opportunities to the community arts administrators who work in rural and small communities.

I was in my position as a community arts administrator in Boonville, Missouri, for four years before I began to fully understand what it was that I was really doing. Had I known earlier, I probably could have avoided some of the mistakes and miscalculations I made. I would have been much clearer about the resources and skills I needed in order to do my work more effectively. It also would have contributed to my sense of being part of a profession. As a result, I probably would have been much more secure and self-confident in my work. I definitely would have been much more selective in the professional development workshops and conferences I attended.

The emergence of the statewide assemblies system over the past twenty years has begun to address the need for this specialized training and professional development. These are organizations that are designed to provide the technical assistance and professional and organizational development resources needed by the community arts agencies and staff. But unfortunately, many of them face the same funding restrictions and resource limitations as the community arts agencies they serve. Many of these statewide assemblies are dependent on public funding from the NEA and state arts agencies. With this funding source dwindling, some of the essential technical assistance and professional development services statewide assemblies provide to the field are dwindling as well. The future of these statewide assemblies is a critical issue facing our profession and our field.

One of the values driving community arts development is the contribution it makes to leader-development. Sometimes this is referred to as "democratization of the arts." It acknowledges that the individual and his/her opportunity to participate in the arts on a personal basis is an essential element of who they are as people. It is a way of developing the "citizen artist." It also understands that the sharing of this process of individual self-expression with the larger community population brings about an opportunity for the individual to emerge in a new and more assertive leadership capacity. If community arts development does anything, it invites and enables change. And, if there is anything rural and small communities are resistant to, it is change. The community arts development process challenges individuals and communities to address conflict and resolve it. This was what I didn't know and didn't understand when I started my work in Boonville. I thought I was working to introduce the transforming power of the arts to individuals. I knew this could happen because I had experienced the transforming power of art myself. What I didn't understand in the beginning was that when this happens for individuals in a community setting, it invites and sets in motion a whole host of possibilities for a larger community transformation.

And sometimes, when this happens, some people in the community get upset because their power is threatened if things don't "stay the same." The fact is, some people don't like anything that encourages democratization because it encourages individuals to begin to claim their own power. We need to understand "democratization of the arts" is central to our work as community makers. Engaging in this kind of work is a risky proposition, to say the least, and one that can place the community arts administrator at risk. So, sometimes, we have to gauge our success not by knowing everyone is happy, but rather, knowing some people are uncomfortable. This invites a recognition that perhaps something different has to happen. All of this points to the need for specialized skills in conflict resolution, helping people to address that which makes them uncomfortable in a creative way. Yet, with all of the potential risk, community arts development provides a powerful invitation to individual and community transformation. It is for these reasons we need to find ways to better equip and train individuals and organizations to do community arts development work in the unique context of the rural and small community setting.

Therefore, our job is to create the opportunity for individuals to participate in the arts on a personal basis. What happens after that is out of our hands. We must honor art in and of itself. What we need to recognize is that as the individual expresses himself/herself through the arts, there is also an invitation to participate in the democratization of the arts - the arts as an expression and experience of community leadership. This is the heart and soul of the community arts development process. Alfred Arvold recognized it back in 1923, when he talked about the arts as leadership in country communities. Robert Gard understood it when he talked about the arts as that which alter the face and heart of America. Baker Brownell understood it when he wrote about art as action, stating that art is for the value of doing art.

Obstacles to Community Arts Development in Rural and Small Communities

Traditionally, there are two problems people consistently talk about as being obstacles to community arts development in rural and small communities. These have been generalized into two categories: lack of funding and low audience participation. Unfortunately, this is a generalization and does a disservice to most communities. It fails to take into account the possibility that these problems are only symptoms of a more basic, underlying problem - a lack of understanding of the unique role and value of arts in the rural area and small community setting. As stated earlier, lack of understanding exists not only by those in the community who do not support the programs and services of the community arts agencies, but also by many of those who work in the agencies themselves. And, it also exists for many commissioned with the responsibility of overseeing state and national funding support for the agencies and their programs. This is one of the reasons community arts programming receives such a small percentage of the public funding dollar.

This lack of understanding is based on a preconceived notion of the role of art, ignoring the fact that art for the smaller community may not be the same as it is for the larger communities because it exists in a different context. It is an attitude and value often imposed from the outside, expecting community arts agencies in rural and small communities to do the traditional arts programming (music, dance, theatre, etc.) and to be the primary delivery system for art that is brought to them from outside the community. This ruralism results in a limited view of the potential that exists within these communities themselves.

And, even when there are innovative and creative efforts by these agencies in rural and small communities to break through this traditional understanding of art, they run into the barrier of the community they are serving not understanding and/or outside support agencies imposing their attitudes and values in order to have them qualify for funding and technical assistance support. With the decreased public funding support for the arts available to these communities (many of which have not received large amounts of public funding anyway), we find many programs folding or downsizing to the point where they can't fulfill what they believe to be their role in the community. While this certainly has its downside, I am convinced it might well be the very impetus and catalyst that is needed for people to focus on the real work of community arts development. This has never been dependent on public funding. If fact, there have been few public funded programs that understand this work. Now is the time we can focus on the community arts development process and the real role of the arts in the community setting. It is an opportunity for all of us to rethink our work, redesign our organizations, and reinvent ways to get it done. It is an invitation for us to be creative again. And that is an invitation that is, for many of us, long overdue. Recognizing the unique context of arts in rural and small communities, as well as the role and values of the community arts experience in this context, is critical to insure successful community arts development.

A lot of attention is being paid to "rural issues" in the arts community these days. In fact, the struggle and future of rural and small communities increasingly has become part of our national dialogue. And rightly so. Our communities are at risk, especially our rural and small communities. We are in a time of change and transition and a lot of people are afraid. People know our communities are in trouble, but they don't know why. Those of us involved in community-making through the community arts development process know one of the reasons - our communities are disintegrating because we have lost part of the "common sense" that is necessary to keep them together. And one of the sources of identifying, conserving, celebrating, and transmitting this "common sense," is the arts.

It is time we realize that rural areas and small communities are more than just depressed communities and struggling organizations with enormous problems. Yes, there are problems, but there are also incredibly innovative organizations doing creative and exciting things in communities all over this country. It is rural genius in action and it has enormous potential to change and transform individuals and communities. We have evidence of this. We know this is true.

This raises several important issues. First, it indicates there is as much work to be done outside the communities as there is within them. This is especially true as it relates to creating a shared language to discuss who we are, what we do, and why we do it. Second, if we are going to provide the resources for our communities to survive, it means that strengthening the community arts development process in rural and small communities ought to be the number one priority of public and private funding agencies.

Third, we have to recognize that community arts development requires training to develop the specialized skills necessary for us to work in the unique context of rural and small communities. This means changing our attitude concerning the important role and responsibility of community arts administrators by not viewing these positions as entry level jobs requiring little or no experience. It also means that the most essential skill we need to develop is being able to effectively communicate the values of the arts in rural and small communities. This means knowing that the arts are more than entertainment. It means understanding that the arts can nurture the lives of everyone, serving as a catalyst and a change agent that makes the arts a vital part of the community arts development process. And it means communicating these roles and values to everyone with whom we work.

We need to be inventive and innovative in finding new ways and new systems to accomplish these tasks. We've got to be willing to take some risks. If the rural and small communities we serve can take risks (and believe me, they do every day), then so can those of us who work with them.

The arts are an industry, they do have an economic impact-yes. But that is not why the arts exist. That is a side result, an indirect benefit. It is a benefit shared by any program that receives public funding. It is a traditional advocacy argument whose effectiveness is decreasing. What we have to convince people of is that the arts touch people's lives. First and foremost, the arts are an expression of what it means to be human. In the context of rural and small communities, the arts are an expression of human beings engaged in the act of creating the human community. It is an exciting and exhilarating experience that can change lives and humanize structures. It is a special process that takes place in a unique context. In rural and small communities, celebrating cultural democracy through creative expression is an art in and of itself. This is why community-making through the community arts development process contributes significantly to rebuilding the front porch of America.

The *New Janusians*
Ode to the Community Makers

We are the new Janusians,
gifted and cursed with the ability to look both ways -
never turn, never move - yet clearly see
both the start and the end at the same time.
Driven to unravel the mystery, we revel
in the genius of simple-complexity.
Sometimes lost in the confusion of creative chaos,
we are guided by the clear sense of direction
that comes from knowing we are not clear
about what it is we see.

We are the stand aparts,
filled with a longing to be a part of
yet knowing we will always be apart from,
just a little -
making community wherever we go,
inviting everyone to be a part yet knowing
when they arrive we will already be gone.

We are driven by the passion,
moved by the mission of community-making.
Forged in fire, fused by flame,
we are the candle burning at both ends,
and, sometimes, in the middle -
not by choice, but by the DNA buried deep
in the marrow of our bones -
knowing the circle will not be whole
until we step over that threshold,
cross the line between what is and what is yet to be,
dreamthinking what is not but still a possibility.

We are awe struck by the capacity of life.
Knowing the power of the sense of place
we make sense of who we are
by making common sense -
by making community.

Always making community.

Public Trust?

*The Ethical Crisis Facing Nonprofit, Tax-Exempt,
Cultural Institutions in America*

*As a community arts developer, I have attended a lot of
interesting meetings. There was one meeting in particular I
have never forgotten. I was working with a community arts
administrator who was having difficulty with some of the
members of the board of directors. This person's background
wasn't in nonprofit work but rather in public, government
service. This person was unfamiliar, and uncomfortable, with
the structure and process of the nonprofit, community-based
organization. I had been working with this individual to
develop strategies to help the board address their
responsibilities as trustees of the organization. I was invited
by the administrator to attend a meeting with the Executive
Committee. It was to be informal meeting with just a few
people. When I arrived at the meeting, the room was filled to
capacity. There must have been over forty people there.
Obviously, something was going on, I just didn't know what.*

*Once the meeting started, it did not take long for it to
digress into a full-fledged, organizational crisis. As a guest
at the meeting, I was in no position to intervene (although, I
have always suspected this is why the arts administrator
invited me to attend the meeting). Before an hour had passed,
the arts administrator had resigned and left the meeting. The
treasurer had given a report, indicating that the organization
was over $25,000 in debt and announced that the
organization had not paid FICA for over two years. The most
stunning revelation of all was that all of this was apparently
a surprise to the board of directors. They were indignant.
They placed all of the blame on the administrator, ignoring
the fact that, as the board of directors, they were actually the
ones responsible for the debt and the failure to report to the
IRS. None of the people in that room realized the extent to
which the organization had violated the public trust by failing
to be good stewards of public funds. The sad thing is that this
is not as uncommon a situation as we would like to think.*

Up to this point, we have been focusing on communities and why they are at risk. Now I want to take this one step further by stating that the very organizations we are using to try and address these problems - our cultural, value-teaching, community-based, nonprofit organizations - may be at risk themselves. The traditional community-based, nonprofit, tax-exempt organizational structure that has been the major vehicle for our work in community-making may not be in the best shape for the work it is doing. One of the reasons for this is these organizations are susceptible to the values collisions of which I spoke earlier.

Sometimes these community conflicts result in organizational structures that lose their value center - that is, they lose touch with the core values that brought them into existence. When this happens, it can produce a values violation that contradicts the very reason the organization came into existence in the first place. One of the problems we have in addressing nonprofit organizations is the fact we rarely talk about values. Yet, our most successful for-profit corporations are absolutely clear that they must be value-centered. And, ironically, many of the core values these corporations use to increase productivity and their profit margins come right out of the nonprofit sector. The most successful corporations are people-centered and service-centered. This includes more than the customers who buy their products. This emphasis on values also includes the very people within these corporations responsible for producing the products that customers purchase.

Values are a very difficult thing to talk about. When we talk about values, we are talking indirectly about ethics, for ethics are systems of principles derived from a specific value orientation. That is, our ethics are how we act out our values. Therefore, as we explore ways to strengthen nonprofit, tax-exempt organizations, I propose two ideas for consideration. First, it is necessary to focus on organizational values, since you cannot have an ethical organization if its actions are inconsistent with its values. Second, it is important to pay particular attention to the values of those cultural organizations that are among the primary sources of identifying, conserving, celebrating, and transmitting the cultural values of our society. I refer to these as "value teaching" institutions, and I include in this category the cultural institutions of religion, higher education, and arts/ humanities organizations. These all fit into the unique category of nonprofit, tax-exempt organizations. Combined, these institutions have an enormous impact on the development of values in our society. Yet, when one examines them closely, it is clear that these "value-teaching" institutions are facing an ethical crisis of their own. The thesis of this essay is that this ethical crisis very well may be inherent in the nonprofit, tax-exempt status of these organizations and threatens their very existence. This problem is not insurmountable, but it is a problem we have failed to address and cannot ignore any longer. This is especially true if predictions are correct that we are moving toward a third sector, community-service based economy.

The Nonprofit Organization - Public Trust or Public Trough?

As our society moves steadily toward a service-based economy, it is likely nonprofit, tax-exempt organizations will not only increase in number but also social and political importance. These organizations have unique structures, are volunteer based, and most important of all, are tax-exempt. The Internal Revenue Service 501 (c) (3) tax-exemption category is a much sought after and coveted designation. It has three very important financial benefits for the organizations that receive it. First, they do not pay taxes on anything they make as income as long as it is within IRS regulations. Second, people and businesses can make a cash or in-kind donation to these organizations and have that gift be tax-deductible from their federal taxes. Third, these organizations are eligible for the vast array of public funding programs and grants made available by the federal government and private organizations with these nonprofit designations. When you combine these tax-exempt benefits with the availability of federal programs and grant monies, there is an enormous advantage to being tax-exempt. Few tax-exempt organizations understand the full range of benefits they receive. In fact, there are many who maintain they are not accountable to IRS regulations because they do not seek public federal programs or grant monies. What they fail to recognize is the tax-exempt benefits are, in effect, indirect public funding. They also fail to realize that with this privilege comes public accountability. Or, as identified in the title of this essay, public trust.

The nonprofit sector is currently undergoing enormous change. Questions are being asked about nonprofits by government and nonprofit officials alike. It wasn't all that long ago that Congress invited the AARP (American Association of Retired People) and the NRA (National Rifle Association) into Congressional Committee for questioning. Both organizations were directly challenged for alleged violations of their IRS tax-exempt status. With as much clout as the AARP and NRA have, can the rest of the nonprofit sector in our country be far behind? On what basis can we assume we will escape this scrutiny?

The federal government is running out of places to raise revenue. It has cut programs about as much as it can. There is only one source of revenue left - the third sector. Nonprofit institutions in the United States are the single largest wealth holders in the country. There are literally billions of dollars lost to general government revenue because of the nonprofit, tax-exempt status. There are many people in the government who believe there are too many nonprofit organizations. They also believe many of them are in violation of their tax-exempt status. And they may be correct. There are also those in our society who believe many nonprofit organizations have become so consumed by the loss of revenue they have become more interested in their own survival than in meeting people's needs.

I would add two more concerns to the list. First, are some nonprofit organizations abusing the public trust by viewing their tax exemption as a ticket to the public funding trough? Second, are some nonprofit groups creating programs simply to get public funding, risking a contradiction of their organizational values in order to survive? My answer to these questions is a resounding yes! I believe this is the source of the ethical crisis that threatens the future of these value-teaching organizations, and potentially, the moral fabric of our society as a whole. This is very much the case for community-based, nonprofit, tax-exempt organizations doing community arts development work.

The Ethical Crisis Facing Nonprofit, Tax-Exempt Cultural Organizations

According to IRS regulations, there is legal accountability that goes with the privilege of tax-exemption. Or, at least, there is supposed to be. A very good case could be made that this accountability is increasingly being ignored and/or violated by nonprofit organizations. It is not necessarily that they are doing it on purpose, but it is happening just the same.

In recent years, we have witnessed example after example of the violation of public trust. One merely needs to remember the enormity of the recent research scandal at Stanford University, where federal funds were diverted for use in areas unrelated to the purpose of the grants. Tremors from the abuse of funds by United Way continue to rock the nonprofit world, years later. And, as we prepare to go to press with this publication, the Speaker of the House, Newt Gingrich, has been found guilty by the House Ethics Committee for mixing contributions to tax-exempt organizations with partisan activities to further his political goals. As a result of these ethics violations, he received an unprecedented reprimand from the full House. I could spend the rest of this essay citing examples of abuse of tax-exempt status that violate the public trust.

The fact is, historically entrusted to promote cultural values, some of our most important cultural, value-teaching institutions are actually contributing to the loss of the very values they are supposed to be teaching. It is easy to ascertain that this behavior is unethical. But, when we acknowledge the role these institutions play in identifying, conserving, celebrating, and transmitting cultural values, it raises an alarming question as to exactly what kind of values these organizations are teaching or promoting. This potential values collision threatens the organizational culture of these cultural organizations. To understand this threat, we need to look at two kinds of "values collisions," external and internal.

The External Values Collision

The external "values collision" occurs when an organization's values are challenged from outside the organization. Nonprofit organizations seeking public funding often find themselves confronted with the ethical dilemma of whose value system the public funding is designed to support. Each nonprofit organization is created for a specific purpose, designed to serve a particular and, many times, exclusive constituency. Yet, without tax exemption, many of these organizations could not exist. Therein lies the problem. Whose mission takes precedence: the organization seeking the funding or the agency giving the funding that is designed to meet the needs of the public? To get the public monies, an organization agrees to serve the public; when in reality, they may be only serving the needs of their membership. At a minimum, this raises concern about the ability of some organizations to be true to their own organizational values and still meet the mandate of public funding and public trust. Let me cite a few examples.

It was only a few years ago when a gallery at a state university received public funding to mount a retrospective exhibition of photographer Robert Mapplethorpe. Included in the exhibition were the famous "seven photographs" that set off a public furor that resulted in the pornography, obscenity, and censorship battles between the evangelical religious and political right and the National Endowment for the Arts. Unfortunately, this controversy is still going on today. The issues, public/community standards versus freedom of expression and individual rights, are still unresolved and the source of conflict in our society. It is interesting to note, the evangelical religious and political right, the major opponent fighting against public funding for the arts, uses the same tax-exempt status to support their "advocacy/ lobbying" efforts to fight the arts. This raises a question as to whether or not they are, in effect, using public funding to impose their values on the public. In essence, doing the very same thing they accuse the arts of doing, promoting their views by using federal funds.

Institutions of higher education find themselves confronted with a similar conflict relating to issues surrounding cultural diversity. No public or private institution receiving public funding can fail to address the need for cultural inclusion. While the call for cultural inclusion is clear, the way to accomplish it is not. For private colleges and universities that are church-related (and many of them are), the issue of cultural diversity becomes an even more difficult issue to resolve. They face the same issues as religious institutions. That is, how to remain true to the sectarian values that brought them into existence (which by definition are exclusive) and still be culturally diverse. These are perplexing issues that clearly result in a "values collision," confronting these institutions with the choice of staying true to their organizational values or jeopardizing their public funding.

Doing what needs to be done to qualify for public funding sometimes makes it difficult for organizations to be true to their values. In addition, there are times when the evaluation criteria and restrictions placed on funding eligibility forces the organization to change in order to comply. Unfortunately, the need for financial support frequently wins out in these situations, and another "values collision" occurs.

Finally, a values collision may occur when public funding agencies intervene in private organizations. More than once, I have witnessed intervention by public funding agencies into organizational matters. This ends up dramatically altering the nature of the organization by requiring it to change or do something that violates its core purpose and values. This is especially true when an organization, by definition of its purpose, takes on an adversarial role with the very agency from which it is seeking funding. It is not unusual for public funding to be used as a "leverage" to force the organization to "tow the line", or punish it for not doing so by reducing or denying funding. While clearly unethical, a system as unregulated as public funding of nonprofit, tax-exempt organizations, frequently invites this political abuse.

The Internal Values Collision

I believe there is an internal "values collision" that is inherent in nonprofit, tax-exempt values-teaching cultural organizations. It occurs when the organizational culture of cultural organizations is challenged from within. My experience has been that many individuals involved in nonprofit, tax-exempt organizations have little or no knowledge or understanding of the values that brought their organization into existence and/or currently drive its mission. Consequently, these organizations do not have a strong value center from which they make decisions. They lack an evaluation document that can be used as a standard for what is and what is not appropriate to do and be consistent with their values. Without this value standard, they can't make informed decisions. In addition to this, there are conflicting beliefs about the organizational values by individuals within the same organization. This creates an internal "values collision" that rarely gets addressed, let alone resolved.

Something else that is happening at an alarming rate is the emergence of what I call the "nonprofit corporate raider." That is, someone with a strong personality and personal agenda comes into an organization, finds a leadership vacuum, takes over, and imposes a personal value system that supersedes that of the organization. Ironically, this happens most frequently and quite legally in the quiet but socially accepted, *coup d'etat* of the annual election meeting of officers. My experience is, this happens before anyone in the organization figures out what is really going on. Unfortunately, by then it is usually too late.

Finally, because of the enormous responsibility placed on paid administrators in nonprofit organizations, and the fact many of these organizations have the lowest paying salaries, there is a high amount of stress, burnout, and staff turnover. In addition, many individuals who sit on the boards of directors of nonprofit organizations frequently have no training and/or preparation to handle this kind of responsibility. When this is combined with the fact that few people, paid and non-paid staff and volunteers, know or understand the organization's values, we end up with organizations that are inadequately managed and ineffective stewards of public and, many times, private funds. The end result of all of this is, the organizational culture of many cultural organizations is in crisis. They find themselves at odds with the very reason they came into existence. This creates an internal "values collision" that causes a gradual disintegration of the organization's core values. This produces an organization that is uncentered, creating an imbalance and instability that goes unnoticed until the organization faces dissolution.

Practice Strategies for Avoiding the "Values Collision"

When a nonprofit organization finds itself facing either an internal or external "values collision," it makes it difficult to be ethically centered and balanced. My experience has been that most organizations are experiencing both collisions. This is especially true in rural and small communities. In the final portion of this essay, I am going to introduce three specific "practice strategies" to address the ethical crisis confronting nonprofit cultural institutions. The essay on Navigating White Water in a Leaky Raft will apply these practice strategies specifically to the community arts agency.

1. Kick the Public Funding Fix; Break the Addiction

Public funding is addictive. It is very easy for nonprofit organizations to build a dependency on it and be unable to function without it. The smaller the organization, the more likely this is to be the case. The smaller the organization, the less money it takes to become dependent. I believe some public funding agencies like it this way because this is a form of indirect control. I have seen entire organizational budgets and programs created solely to meet an external funding request guideline. There certainly can be a "high" produced when we get public funding. Many people view this as an official "certification." After all, organizations don't get funded unless they are qualified. But, is this really true?

The bottom line is this funding high can be addictive. There used to be enough money around to support this habit. The world has changed. Public funding is scarce. Unfortunately, instead of focusing on alternative sources of support, the concern for survival and maintaining the habit takes over. From that point on, everything the organization does becomes self-serving.

Decisions that are made on programming and budgeting become "profit/funding" motivated, rather than "process/purpose" motivated. As a result, the organization becomes internally focused while being externally driven. I believe the ethical organization must be just the opposite - externally focused (service) and internally driven (values). Kicking the public funding fix is the first step toward accomplishing this goal.

Public funding is not, in and of itself, a problem. Our potential dependency on this funding is a problem. Therefore, the funding crisis - the reduction of public money - isn't the problem, it's the symptom. I believe people put their money where their values are. I have recently revised this statement to say people put their "capital" where their values are. And, in nonprofit organizations, the most important source of capital is human capital (time).

Our job is not only to be clear about our values but to also make sure we communicate these values to the world around us every chance we get. We also need to be sure we communicate these values to those people within our organization. If we do this, if we are clear about our values and communicate them effectively, the money will be there to support our work. If we don't, we will end up with financially unstable and potentially unethical organizations that will not survive this values collision. Shared values and shared vision is the answer.

2. Organizational Reframing: Develop The "Third View"

The world has changed, and with it, so has the approach to organizational structure has changed as well. Ironically, the "for-profit" corporate giants long ago recognized the change that was needed and began creating new and innovative organizational "systems" to adapt to it. Nonprofit corporations, on the other hand, continue to use the outdated and archaic structures that most of the for-profit corporations abandoned a long time ago. It is time for cultural organizations to focus on their organizational cultures and reframe the way we approach our structure and governance. What we need to do is to think of our organizations in a completely new way.

There are numerous ways to accomplish this task. One of the first things we have to do is to acknowledge that organizational culture exists. We have to look at our purpose and clarify our organizational values. This can be accomplished through a values assessment or values audit. This is not just asking the question, "Who are we?", but the follow-up question as well, "Why are we this way?" It isn't just looking at what we do, it examines why we do it. In addition, it examines whether or not the "asserted" values (what we say we do) are consistent with "acted out" values (what we actually do).

Once this is done, we then need to develop an organizational system (as opposed to structure), that clarifies how each component of the organization functions and relates to the core values of the organization. This system is not based on the traditional vertical or horizontal flow chart. This requires a "third view," because it requires an entirely new perspective to see it. It is not vertical, or horizontal (one dimensional). Instead, it is circular or spherical (three-dimensional), much like the essential element of life itself, the cell. The best physical model I have come up with to portray this concept is the gyroscope. In a gyroscope, everything moves except the center - the core, it stays stationary. Using this as a model, the core of an organization consists of the value(s) that drive its existence. Everything is connected to this value core (core value). When we look at our organizational systems as living organisms - consisting of people who are communicating with each other - we can then create an organizational map that lets people know how to get to where they have to go to make things work. And, do so in an ethical way that honors the values driving the organization and its work.

3. The Death of Superman: Rethinking Leadership

Many nonprofit organizations have governance systems that are archaic and perilously out of touch with current trends in organizational theory. They perpetuate a traditional style of leadership that is based on position. I call this the "Superman

Syndrome," and it is perpetuated by the continuing and mistaken belief that one individual can "save" an organization. What it does is encourage autocratic decision making that may achieve the end product desired, but violates the value-centered process. When this happens, regardless of how good the end product is, it makes organizational integrity difficult, if not impossible. It also inevitably contributes to the ethical "dis-integration" of the organizational culture because it has lost its connection to the core value(s). The more frightened and threatened an organization becomes, the more vulnerable it is to this type of manipulative leadership. It is time to retire the "Big Red S" and encourage a new kind of leadership.

This is specifically addressed to those who serve in administrative positions in nonprofit organizations. But this requires rethinking the role of leadership. Our job as administrators is not to drive the organization, but to promote the shared values that drive the organization. I believe ethical leadership, therefore, is value-centered. Ethical leadership keeps the process and the product of an organization in a healthy, creative balance. I also believe ethical leadership engages in the "leadership of discomfort," inviting and enabling individuals and organizations to face conflict and resolve it (not something that is easily done in rural and small communities). Finally, I believe ethical leadership is grounded in the organization's values and manifests the courage to take risks, to innovate, and to try new things to meet the growing needs of the communities we serve.

Conclusion

Nonprofit cultural institutions - in particular, religious, higher education, and arts/humanities organizations - play a very important role in teaching values. But, many of these organizations are confronted with an ethical crisis that threatens to diminish the contribution they make. As we address the needs of these organizations, I believe we must carefully examine the role of organizational values and the role these values play in the organizational culture of these cultural organizations. For the simple fact remains, we cannot cultivate ethical organizations if we are not ethical ourselves. To fail to do this is to fail to fulfill the only justification we have for public support of what we do - the public trust. We have not always been mindful of this trust. If we are going to have a future, we had better begin to pay attention to this. Without question, this is the single greatest challenge facing community arts organizations. To face this challenge, we are going to have to learn how to navigate through the turbulence of crisis, change, and transition.

Navigating White Water in a Leaky Raft
Organizations Facing Change and Transition

White water rapids - the image brings to mind the thrill, the adventure, and the challenge of navigating a raging river. It appeals to creative, innovative, quick-thinking, high-energy people. This certainly is a fitting way to talk about those of us involved in community arts development. If our lives have been anything in the past decade, they have been on a fast, exhilarating ride down the white water rapids of change and transition. Why not? We are used to doing it - we have done it all of our lives. We are experts at navigating through the rapids, skilled at missing the rocks. We have done it our entire careers working with nonprofit, community-based organizations. Besides, things couldn't get worse, could they? Well. . .

Anyone who lives in the Midwest, or watched on television in 1993 the Mississippi and Missouri rivers breaking through the man-made levees and flooding land claimed for farming and living, knows the power of water turned enemy. Nature doesn't always respect the limits we place on it. We can't control white water turbulence created by flooding rivers. This is certainly the case for those of us who work in community-making. The environment in which we work is as turbulent now as it has ever been and it shows no signs of letting up. And, while we are excellent navigators, we can't expect to be able to navigate this white water turbulence in a leaky raft. We can't navigate and patch holes at the same time without courting disaster. Up to this point we have "managed" to stay afloat because we were creative, energetic, and willing to take risks. The cost of risk-taking has gone up. So has the price we pay when we fail.

The raft we are navigating is the nonprofit, community arts agency - and this raft has holes in it. Our funding base is decreasing, we have dwindling audiences, a diminishing volunteer pool, too much to do and too little time to do it in, overworked paid-staff, overworked and untrained non-paid staff, and enough religious and political controversy and infighting to keep us totally preoccupied. And, as though all of this crisis, change, and transition weren't enough, the very organizational structure we used to build our raft in the first place may have a flaw in its design. Its structural integrity may not hold up to the increasing stress created by the white water turbulence surrounding us.

The title of this essay is based on a workshop I created in 1992 to help boards, staff, and volunteers of community-based organizations address the issues of crisis, change, and transition facing them. I always begin this workshop with an exercise to help participants identify the white water they find themselves having to navigate. The size and magnitude of the list never fails to astound those involved in the workshop. They know things are difficult, but they have never stopped to assess just how difficult they really are.

Identifying the White Water Turbulence

People know something has changed over the past few years but they can't always put their finger on what it is that has changed. When I work with organizations, I start out by having

them list the white water turbulence in which they find themselves
and their organizations. The following list is a composite list of
the workshops I have presented over the past five years. I have
actually reduced the overall list by combining various areas that
are similar or duplicative. Take a look at the list and see how
many with which you can identify:

Decreasing number of volunteers
Difficult to stay the course
People devalue what it is they do
Communicating in a time of change
Lack of advocacy for artists and their practice
Working with volunteers
Dysfunctional organizational structure
Don't know where our council fits
We don't have a clear "cultural language"
Do not know our history/we are ahistorical
We lack a "shared language" in the arts
Little or no arts in education
Time management
Public accountability
Issues surrounding aesthetic judgement
Attendance is shrinking
We change volunteer leadership too often
Lack of business sense
Over reactive management styles
Too much business sense/lack of art
Volunteers don't know what staff does
Can't recruit/keep board members
Lack of training for board, staff, volunteers
Lack of training that relates to our work
Maintaining organizational integrity
Not getting grants/getting grants
Lack of self-confidence, self-esteem
What we have to do to get grants
People in the community don't know what
  we are doing
We don't tell people what we are doing
People in the community don't know
  why we are doing what we do

This is not a complete list, but it is certainly representative of the various concerns people have regarding the environment in which they are working. One interesting note; the list does not seem to change very much when I am working with an all-volunteer group as opposed to a group that has paid-staff. Apparently the turbulence is the same, regardless. One thing I have never done is to do a white water turbulence listing with a group of just community arts administrators. I suspect the list might be more detailed and a lot longer.

One of the things I have learned during the workshops is to leave plenty of time for people to talk about this list. For many of the participants, it is the first time they have seen all of this in one place and it is a bit overwhelming. There is a lot of change and transition going on - and almost all of it is out of their control. This is a great source of stress - both personal and organizational. Our nonprofit, community-based, arts agency world is not the same as it was even five or ten years ago. It has changed so rapidly none of us can keep up with it. Owning up to the change and transition as well as the individual/organizational stress it creates, is an essential step in helping an organization assess where it is and chart a new course for its future.

Inspecting The Leaky Raft

The problem we have is that we are not just navigating white water. If that was all we had to focus on, we could probably manage to survive the rapids. Our problem is we are navigating the white water rapids in a raft that has holes in it. We can navigate, and we can patch holes. What we can't do very easily is navigate and patch holes at the same time. If we navigate and don't patch the holes, we will sink. If we stop to patch the holes, we are likely going to lose control of the raft and hit the rocks. Most community arts administrators I know are good - but none are able to do both at the same time.

Our organizations aren't designed to take the kind of external and internal pressure they are experiencing. The nonprofit organizational structure has never been easy to understand and it has some inherent design flaws that make it difficult to manage, even by the best of board/administrator teams. It's bad enough to have to deal with the holes caused by the white water rapids, but when they are caused by the organizational structure itself, this creates an entirely different problem to address. We can't keep blaming our problems on everything and everyone else outside the organization - we are causing some of the problems ourselves.

Let's look at the condition in which we find ourselves. First of all, the white water is faster and stronger than it has ever been before. Second, we are not in the raft by ourselves. We are an organization of people and we are not only responsible for navigating ourselves in the raft, but we are responsible for them as well. Third, and perhaps worst of all, we are springing leaks all over the raft. The rafts we are using are old. They have been in the water a long time. The raft has bounced off a lot of rocks and is worn, used, stretched thin. And, just about the time we think we should be hitting the shallows and coasting along (after all, isn't that the reward of a long, white water ride?), we find ourselves facing a long new stretch of white water rapids and we have already taken on too much water.

We cannot control the white water turbulence - this is a given and it is the same for everyone. It is outside our control. We are going along for the ride whether we like it or not. What we can control, is whether or not our raft is ready for the ride. This is a decision that is not beyond our control. But it isn't an easy one to make. Most people don't want to invest the time or energy to fix organizational problems. We think it is self-serving. We think it takes us away from our original mission. The real reason is most of us don't know how to do it.

How do we fix the leaks? Well, the first thing we have to do is find them. And we can't do this in the middle of the rapids. We have to pull out. Sometimes, an organization has to take time to focus on itself. One of the great myths of the nonprofit organization is the fact we don't think our organizational issues merit attention. We think our business is service - and that is what we should be doing, providing service. But, it doesn't take much for the issues of an organization to get in the way of delivering this service - whatever that service may be.

Sometimes pulling out, resting, and renewing ourselves and our organizations is all that is needed - it is an excellent way to address the stress. Ironically, there are those in our society who seek solace and comfort from the white water of their lives by participating in the very things our organizations provide - the nurturing, healing, comforting, energizing power of the arts. Unfortunately, many of us who help make these kinds of experiences available for others, don't have the luxury of enjoying what it is we are inviting them to experience. We who make community by making art available for others, often fail to gain the very benefit everyone gets by participating in and experiencing the arts. We pay a big price for this as well.

After we identify the leaks, we have to develop a strategy to fix them. This is also hard for us to do. Few of us, administrators and volunteers alike, are "structural engineers." Fewer of us are organizational experts. And, unfortunately, most people who do provide resources for organizational development don't always understand the significant aspects and unique differences of nonprofit organizations and the values that drive our work. This is especially true for community arts agencies located in rural and small communities.

Reviewing Our Nonprofit Organizational Structure

If we keep getting leaks in our raft, perhaps we should consider a new raft. Or, maybe the raft is fine, we just need to design it a little differently. But we have to do something. If, as some are saying, we are moving toward a third sector, community service-based economy, the question we must ask ourselves is whether or not we are prepared for this. Are our organizations stable and strong enough to perform in this environment? I am not sure we can answer yes to these questions. Perhaps it is time for us to revisit the nature of our nonprofit, tax-exempt status and determine if there is a way to improve and/or alter this design.

There is another alternative - perhaps not all rural and small community arts agencies need to be tax-exempt. Perhaps the nonprofit status is all that is needed. Some of them may not even need to incorporate as nonprofit. Perhaps some of them don't even need to be formally organized - a partnership or umbrella relationship with another organization could accomplish what they want to do. Or, even more novel, would be to consider the option of being a "for-profit" organization, relying on our own ability and devices to succeed. This may sound extreme, but that doesn't mean we shouldn't explore these and other options available to us. What we shouldn't continue to do is to have blind loyalty to something that may not meet our needs in the first place. It may be time to rethink, reinvent, and redesign what it is we are doing and how we are going about getting it done.

What other corporate structure could survive running the way we run things? We have an organization that is run by a volunteer boards of directors, hardly any of whom are directly acquainted with and/or understand community arts agency theory or practice. We have presidents and executive committee teams that are in existence for two years at the most and then are changed, leaving no consistent leadership. The business of our organization is conducted by volunteer chairpersons, hardly any of whom are trained to do what it is they are doing, yet frequently in complete control or worse, left to their own devices because they haven't been given any training. And these are the people responsible for oversight and managing the volunteers who make up the committees that do the major work of the organization. Most of them aren't trained either.

Perhaps somewhere in this mix is the arts administrator (paid or non-paid). Hardly any of us who are administrators have figured out exactly what our role is in this confusing organizational design. Unfortunately, no one else in the organization has either. Successful single discipline arts organizations have traditionally revolved around the vision of an artistic director. Community arts agencies aren't single discipline organizations. But, we do many of the same things, including producing and presenting. During my dissertation research, I formed a list of functions for which arts administrators were responsible. It was a formidable list indeed. It included the following list:

Grant writing	*Volunteer recruitment*
Grant administration	*Volunteer development*
Grant final reporting	*Exhibit design*
Development of programs	*Exhibit installation*
Public relations	*Technical assistance*
Financial management	*Maintenance*
Bookkeeping/clerical	*Janitorial duties*
Preparation of materials	*Cashier duties*
Fundraising	*Cash management*
Volunteer supervision	*Cash investment*
Newsletter production	*Technical production*
Festival development	*Security management*
Festival management	*Equipment maintenance*
Facility management	

Not only is the diversity of the items on the list staggering, so is the amount of them on the list administrators end up doing. There are few professional positions in this country that demand this number of different administrative skills. And, as I also pointed out, many of us come to our community arts agency positions with little or no experience in administration or nonprofit organizational development. Add to this dynamic that it is our responsibility as administrators to navigate the white water turbulence in an organizational raft that is full of holes. No wonder administrators are stressed out and some, perhaps, bordering on the edge of burnout.

We have an unwieldy structure that is unclearly defined. And somewhere in the picture we have staff (paid and non-paid), usually one person, usually part-time, trying to provide administrative assistance to see that all of this runs smoothly. If this doesn't make you tired, it should. This is the state of affairs in which we live and work on a daily basis. And if you aren't tired and exhausted, it is probably because you have effectively used the survival skill of denial. I am not saying nonprofit organizations are bad. I am not saying I am opposed to the nonprofit organizational classification. In many instances, they are totally appropriate structures. I have seen wonderful organizations defy the odds and do miraculous things. I have worked with organizations like this. There are incredible people doing incredible things in many well structured, functional nonprofit organizations. What I am saying is that this structure may not be for everyone. I am also saying that if we keep the structure, we need to rethink and redesign it. Regardless of what we decide, we have own up to the fact, we have a leaky raft.

Suggestions for Repairing the Raft

We have acknowledged the white water turbulence. We have owned up to the possibility our organizational raft is full of holes. The question we need to answer is, "What can we do about it?". Well, first of all, we have to accept the fact we have little control over the outside turbulence. This is something that affects everyone. It is the environment in which we live. What we can do, is strengthen our organizations so we can be more effective. Hopefully I have made the point about how important our work in community arts development is to rebuilding the front porch of

America. Here are some ideas on how we can strengthen our agencies and organizations and help them get better prepared and equipped to do this work. We must begin by identifying our organizational values, refocus our organizational vision, and define our organizational mission. Once we have done this, we need to change from organizational structures to organizational systems. We need to redefine the role of the administrator as navigator and identify the training and resources needed to help them do their work which includes conflict resolution and issues surrounding cultural diversity.

1. Identify Our Organizational Values

We must identify the values that drive our work. It isn't good enough any more just to say the arts contribute to the quality of life. I am not sure anyone knows what that means anyway. We have to understand the values upon which our work is based, the value of art as expression of the human spirit - the value of art as process.   When we understand this, we can more effectively communicate who we are, what we do, and why we do it. Through this process, people in the community we serve, as well as in our own organizations, will better understand art as a verb, a process people participate in that results in community making. When we do this, people will begin to understand why the arts are an important part of rebuilding the front porch of America.

To accomplish this, we must learn from those who have gone before us, and there are many of them. We need to understand the work the poets, prophets, and pioneers of our field did, and we can do this by learning to read the community maps they left us. We need to take the time to read these maps and reinterpret them for our time, our day, our communities. We also need to do a better job of capturing the work that is being done today. In our own way, we are the poets, prophets, and pioneers who will be the guides for a whole new generation of community makers. We are the map-makers, creating the new maps that will lead the way for generations to come. We have to do a better job of leaving behind the notes and maps others will need to follow our work.

Dealing with values is difficult. Values are part of a culture (in this instance, an organization's culture) and, as such, they are hard to identify and harder to talk about. But, by talking about the values, and identifying the shared values within the organization, we develop a better understanding of what we should be doing and how we should be doing it - that is, our core values. This should result in a value(s) statement that becomes the basis for the organization's evaluation. Everything the organization does, and the way it does it, should be consistent with this "e-value-ation" document. Included in this document should be the organizational vision and mission (see below). It is the most important document the organization has and should guide everything we do.

2. Refocus Our Organizational Vision

Once we have identified the organizational values driving us, we need to identify the organizational vision - that is, where we are going. Far too often, organizational values are unidentified. More frequently, the organizational vision is unclear. We confuse our mission statement as something that provides guidance to us. Most mission statements are little more than generalized statements created in order to satisfy the state requirements to receive nonprofit status. Our organizational vision defines where it is that we are going - the horizon line that defines the nature of our existence by clarifying our goal, our purpose, what we want to accomplish.

Failure to clearly define the vision of the organization can be a major stumbling block to success. Let's return to the metaphor of the raft in white water rapids. Let's assume there are five people in the raft. Let's say each person in the raft is there for a different reason (the "why" they are in the raft). Some are there because they like to take risks. Some are there because they want to learn teamwork. Some are there because they want to get from point A (the launch site) to point B (the final destination) in one piece and with as little turbulence as necessary. If these people don't share the same reason for being in the raft, you are likely to have some discomfort because you can't satisfy all of their expectations. This affects the vision because where you end up and what path you take will depend on the person who has control of the rudder. Without consensus about the trip, everyone will be unhappy (in particular, the person who is trying to steer the raft).

Now, let's look at two different scenarios. First, let's suppose one person has hold of the rudder and is doing the steering. The others are doing the necessary paddling and, when possible, steering with the paddles. The effective rafting experience will have all of these different components working together. Now let's look at a raft that doesn't have one rudder, but five - one for each person in the raft. What we have are a lot of different ideas on where the raft needs to go - and in most white water rapid situations, there isn't a lot of time to discuss this decision. So we have five people who could be making five independent decisions, all of which directly affect the raft. It won't work. It can't work. Failure to identify the path of the raft is equivalent to failing to identify the path and the destination of the organization. There can be multiple values driving your organization, and there usually are - but there must be one, shared vision. Without this, you have very different reasons for being in the same organizational culture.

Failure to have shared values and a clear vision will result in an organizational culture in conflict. This kind of conflict is not one that is easily resolved. My experience has been this type of conflict is the kind that creates crisis. Unfortunately, by the time you get called in to help this type of organization, it is too late to do anything but triage. More unfortunately, nonprofit organizations in rural and small communities are very good at denying conflict. It is not unusual for arts administrators to be hired and quickly discover they are working for a totally different organization than the one they thought they were going to be part of. Identifying a clear organizational vision helps everyone involved to work together in a team to accomplish the same goals.

Organizational vision: without it you have no idea where you are going - your organization is rudderless. The why you exist is the raft; the vision you have is the rudder that guides the raft. You have to have both in order to survive the rapids. The only component of the evaluation document left is the organizational mission.

3. Determine Our Organizational Mission

So, first we identify the values (recognizing those that brought the organization into existence as well as those that are part of your organizational culture now). This helps you recognize that everyone is on board. Second, you refocus the organizational vision and make sure everyone is clear on where you are headed. Third, you determine how you are going to get there. This is the organizational mission. Mission is the most misunderstood of the three.

Simply put, the organizational mission defines how you are going to get to where it is you intend to go. This is the most flexible and changing aspect of an organization. This is what must be revisited on a frequent basis. It does no good to be clear on values (the raft) and the vision (the rudder) if you can't navigate the rapids in the most effective manner possible. In more traditional terminology, the mission is the objectives determined necessary to meet the goals - that is, how we do what we do.

The mission of the organization can't be determined until there is a clear vision and shared values. Everything the organization does must be connected to these first two items on the evaluation document. The mission will greatly influence the design of the organization. Many organizations are created with an inflexible structure. What we need is a flexible structure that can adjust to a changing environment. We have already clearly established the fact that there are more white water rapids than ever before. If we don't create more flexible and adjustable organizational designs, we may not survive the ride. We must find ways to move from inflexible structures to flexible systems. The key to accomplishing this is communication.

4. Change Organizational Design from Structure to System

If you take what I have said in the beginning of this essay seriously, it is likely you are going to be about the issue of organizational change and transition. The likelihood is that you are already experiencing change and transition, you just may not have owned up to it yet. One of the greatest challenges facing you and the organization(s) you serve is communication. It is tough to keep communication channels open when everything around you is in a constant state of change and transition. Structures are rigid, firm, providing clear and definitive boundaries. They help define what is "in" and what is "out." A system, on the other hand, is much more fluid. The purpose of a system is to establish channels of communication so there is no "in" and "out."

From my perspective, there is nothing more important we can do in our field than to find ways to design effective community arts agency organizational systems. To do this, we have to create ways to talk to each other. Open and effective communication is the key. This will help us identify our values, refocus our vision, and determine our mission. When we do this together, we have a balance between effective organizational process and the product we are delivering.

The fact is, most nonprofit, community-based organizations do not have a clear idea of their values, vision, and mission. If that weren't bad enough, even fewer of them have a clear idea of the role a paid administrator plays in all of this (if they have one). And, as frustrating as this may be, my experience has been that not all administrators understand their role either. It is a vicious cycle that ends up in organizational dysfunction, administrator burnout, and community crisis.

The Board of Trustees are stewards of the organizational values. I have intentionally used the term Board of Trustees instead of Board of Directors. The term director is confusing to the nonprofit, volunteer-based organization. The Board is the governance system. Their job as trustees is to serve as stewards of the organizational values and assets. They are not usually involved in the day to day activities and administration of the organization. This is the function of the Administrative Council (usually referred to as the Executive Committee). This is the heart of the management team - and it consists of the officers of the organization and the paid-staff (full-time or part-time). It should operate as a team with everyone on the team assuming their responsibility, clearly defined and consistent with their leadership role in the organization. The purpose of the Administrative Council is to make sure that the programs of the organization (its mission) are consistent with the organizational values and vision. It is then the role of the administrator (paid or non-paid) to enact the decisions and organizational communications of the Administrative Council. To accomplish this, the administrator must work with the volunteers, providing the necessary training and development to ensure the process is working smoothly. It is important to note here that it is not the role of the administrator to do the work, but to make sure that the work gets done. When the administrator ends up doing the work, it circumvents the purpose of the volunteers and eventually renders the organization dysfunctional. It also contributes to the stress and burnout of the administrator, leaving the organization without healthy administrative leadership.

I realize this design is different from the more traditional nonprofit, community-based, organizational structure. This is not just a theoretical design; I have worked with numerous rural and small community organizations to test the model. It works. While the transition to this model is not easy, my experience has been that the end result is a much more compact and efficient design that utilizes the resources (human and financial capital) to their fullest capacity. The time frame for this redesign has never taken less than a year. It requires a lot of organizational development. But, part of the beauty of the design is that it involves the entire membership in the designing process, helping to establish the open communication that is essential for the design itself to work. I realize this is a very limited introduction to a new design concept, but the intent isn't necessarily to promote this one design. It is intended to point out that there are alternative designs that can be used. What we have to do is to begin to explore these alternatives and find one that is the most effective for our own organizations.

The white water turbulence isn't going away. We are going to have to find new ways of supporting our work. This means we won't be able to do everything we have been doing, and this isn't necessarily bad either. It won't hurt us to downsize. In fact, most cultural institutions and arts organizations I know are notorious "program stackers" anyway, refusing to let programs die a dignified death - a kind of self-imposed organizational downsizing. I don't know a single nonprofit, tax-exempt organization that couldn't benefit from this. It is a perfect opportunity to evaluate what is essential and what is the best way to get it done. And, it is important to remember, a system is designed to be flexible.

Therefore, the organization should be reviewing the system on a consistent basis to make sure it is working efficiently. I believe the person who has primary responsibility for doing this is the one whose hand is on the rudder - and this should be the administrator.

5. Redefine the Community Arts Administrator As Navigator

We need to redefine the role of community arts administrators. This role needs to be elevated and viewed with much more importance. We are not managers, we are administrators. I believe our role in the organization is service. We serve the organization, so our organization can serve the community. But this requires rethinking the role of leadership.

Arts administrators are not responsible for the organizational values. Our job is to understand them, promote them effectively, and to make sure they are understood and shared by the entire organization. If an administrator determines the organizational values (and some do), the organization becomes staff-driven rather than board-driven, and this is not healthy. Staff come and go - the organization stays. The values have to be under the stewardship of those who stay. Our role as administrator is not to determine the vision. That has to be shared by the entire organization. What we do is to provide the leadership to see that the values are preserved and communicated, the organizational vision is fulfilled, and the mission is accomplished.

To do this, the administrator must be the navigator - that is, to pilot the organizational craft. In the original meaning of the word, a pilot is the person who had the rudder (the maps) and could read the waters, the wind, and the stars. The pilot wasn't even the one who had control of the steering wheel - but rather guided the one steering. The pilot wasn't the captain - the pilot was the one who could make sure the commands of the captain were carried out. Without the pilot, the ship (or raft) would surely run aground or hit the rocks.

We need to change our understanding of community arts administration from positional leadership (captain) to functional leadership (navigation). We are the ones helping to navigate the white water turbulence. It is our hand that is on the rudder. We had better have a good map and we had better know how to read it.

6. Develop Community Arts Administrator Training Resources

For too long we have not had effective training resources for those of us who work in community arts agencies. We go to conferences where the presenters have little or no idea of what it is we really do. We attend fundraising seminars designed for people in metropolitan cities. We participate in workshop after workshop that totally misses the mark on helping us help our organizations.

Few of us have the training necessary to do this work. Many of us are hired from within the organization itself, having served as a volunteer before we become paid staff. Many of us are part-time and have other responsibilities. Most of us don't know where to go to get the training we need that applies to our particular situations. And, when we do find it, we have to spend most of our time translating it into the context of our own work.

The community coordinators of state arts agencies were resources available to help administrators and community arts agencies function effectively. But their role is limited by the fact that the agency for which they work is a funder of the organizations they are trying to serve. This creates a confusing relationship at the least - and an awkward one at best, because it presents a potential conflict of interest for both.

Statewide assemblies of community arts agencies have been effective in creating training resources geared to the rural and small community situation. But even these service organizations have a problem getting people to their training events. What we have to do is to create a new system of delivering the training resources that our community arts administrators need. And it is vital we understand these resources must be based on the values driving community arts development.

The numerous and multifaceted functions the community arts administrator performs clearly requires specific skills. In addition, we must understand the unique context of this work in rural and small communities. The role of the community arts administrator is a demanding, complicated, and ever-changing position. It is a generalist position that requires a large number of different, specialized skills (remember the list a few pages ago). It is also a position that is quite frequently underrated and misunderstood, by both the organizations and the administrators themselves. It is a difficult position, and it can be a lonely job. There are few people around who really understand what it is we do. The result is we many times end up feeling isolated. With the ever-changing white water turbulence around us, we are likely candidates for an inordinate and unhealthy amount of stress. This, combined with the fact we are a "care giving" profession, makes us likely candidates for burnout. These two factors combined with our sense of isolation, make our need for professional association not only important, but essential.

7. Learn Conflict Resolution Skills

It is very clear that we work in a conflicted environment. Our organizations are full of conflict because of change and transition, and so are the communities in which our organizations exist. Let me add one additional source of conflict - success. If we are successful in doing our work, we have to be prepared for problems.

Sometimes problems arise not because we are doing a bad job, but because we are doing a good job. Participation in the arts can bring about a genuine sense of empowerment for individuals. The arts give a voice to many people who have not known how to communicate this voice before. This can be unsettling to people in positions of power and prestige because being successful community makers brings about what is called the democratization of the arts. This is when the arts can set in motion a transformation not just of individuals but of entire communities. It is a powerful force. I have witnessed it first hand. I watched it happen in Boonville, Missouri. The more we worked with individuals and their own personal transformation, the more it set in motion a larger, community transformation. I was unaware of this indirect outcome of our work and it caught me off guard, creating political problems I didn't understand. I came under political attack from several fronts. For a long time, I was convinced the problems and conflicts were my fault, the result of not doing my work the right way. What I learned, much later on, was the fact that some of the problems were coming about because I was doing a good job - I was being successful. While I most certainly would go about doing some of what I did differently, knowing the potential difficulty it could create, would have better prepared me for what happened. It also would have made my life a lot easier during those hard years in Boonville when I felt isolated and very much alone.

What we need as community arts administrators is a good set of conflict resolution skills. My experience in rural and small communities is that one of the things we do best is conflict denial. This is true in our organizations and in the larger community. Conflict, in and of itself, is not necessarily bad. Change always brings about some conflict. Conflict is bad only when it is ignored, denied, or unattended. Conflict is a warning sign, it is an indication something is wrong. It can be an essential ingredient to the life of a healthy organization (or individual for that matter).

One of the most significant things we could offer our organizations is an effective process of addressing conflict and finding creative ways to reach resolution and reconciliation. This would not only help us in our role as organizational navigators, it would make a significant contribution to our ability to serve as cultural brokers in our communities. It would certainly make us more comfortable in tackling this important issue.

8. Learn to Address Cultural Diversity in an Authentic Manner

Those of us involved in the arts have been addressing diversity for a long time. We have the right words in our vocabulary, but I am not sure we have been effective in understanding what the words mean. Our communities are changing. Cultural diversity isn't something we can ignore. In fact, it may well be those of us involved in the community arts field will find ourselves and our organizations in a position to be "cultural brokers," helping to bring different cultures together. As I discussed earlier in the book, the arts create circles of convergence where people of different cultures gather together.

One of the first things we need to understand is that cultural diversity isn't just a matter of color. There are lots of cultural differences - color, race, religion, gender, age, sexual preference, and ethnicity are just a few. The other thing we have to understand is the fact that there is a lot of resistance in our communities to change - and the issue of diversity seems to have become one of the largest sources of community polarization. The other thing we have to understand is the fact that the arts have always been one of the ways in which these cultural values are identified, conserved, transmitted, and celebrated. This is why we find ourselves in the middle of so much social conflict right now.

What we need are effective intercultural communication skills to help our organizations and members address issues of diversity. We need to understand diversity in all of its challenge and possibilities. It will do us no good if we rebuild the front porch of America and it ends up not being inclusive. We have already been there - it doesn't work. The new front porch must be a place for all people in our community to gather and celebrate who we are. This is the only way the community making process can be authentic. We must view this challenge as one of the most important issues we address. Both as community arts agencies and as professional community arts administrators. And to do this effectively, we need to create effective community partnerships with other cultural organizations. We cannot do this alone. We need to be working with libraries, schools, museums, historical organizations, and institutions of higher education to find ways to address these issues together. We have something significant to offer this process but we need to work with others to get it done. When we find ways to accomplish this task, our communities will be better for it.

Finding the Still Water

These are just a few of the challenges facing those of us who do this work. These are just a few of the possibilities that exist for us to find ways to meet these challenges. There are others. What we must begin to do is to explore these possibilities together and discover which ones work. One way to do this is to find the still water that will allow us the time to do this important organizational work.

It doesn't matter what we call ourselves or how we define the work we do. What matters is that we do the work. Many of our rural and small communities are in crisis. Many of the community arts agencies in these communities are in crisis as well. There isn't time to sit around and wait for someone else to do something for us - we have to act ourselves. Now.

There is a lot of stress out there. We have no choice about addressing change and transition. The white water turbulence shows no signs of slowing down. As a result, it is increasingly critical that our organizational raft be free of leaks. We can't afford the diversion of repairing the raft any longer. We have work to do and we need to focus on the work, not the organizational needs that will end up preventing us from getting the work done.

While we are doing this, we must also own up to the fact that the demands on our time and our energy will not be decreasing any time soon. Our field is aging and we don't have unlimited resources to keep our fires burning. We are people who give a lot and we have given it freely. But we must come to grips with our need to get something back. We are professionals working in a very important profession - community-making. We need to be at our best to do this work effectively.

We have an unprecedented opportunity to do something that will have a lasting impact on our communities and our nation as a whole. If we are successful, the work we do in the rural and small communities we serve will significantly contribute to rebuilding the front porch of America.

Part III

The Relationship Between Arts and Values

Grassroots & Mountain Wings

Reflections On Being A Community Arts Administrator

A few years ago I was talking about my work to the person sitting next to me on an airplane. After we talked a while, he asked me how I got involved in community arts development work. The question startled me. In all the years I had been in the field, I had never been asked that before. I thought for a minute and responded with a somewhat perplexed, "I don't know. I really don't know how I ended up where I am." But then I thought a little more about the question and added with certainty and assurance, "But I do know this - I was very intentional in getting here!"

I think this may be the case for many of us. We may not have consciously chosen a career path that knowingly would bring us to this place, to this profession, to this community-making work. But, most of us are so deeply value-driven by the work we do, it wouldn't matter even if we had consciously chosen something else - we probably would have ended up here anyway.

We talk a lot about the arts - about economic impact, arts as an industry, arts advocacy, criteria of evaluation, artistic excellence, and the role of local arts agencies in all of this. What we don't talk about much is arts in the community and what they do for people.

We talk a lot about arts administration - about management skills, professional development, organizational standards, and best practices. What we don't talk about much is what it means to work in and for the arts in the community.

In fact, we don't use the word "community" much any more. We call ourselves "arts administrators" and our organizational "local arts agencies." Somewhere in the course of the past twenty years, we have begun to lose touch with the word that provided much of the motivation for the pioneering work in our field. We need to reclaim the word because it describes not only the work we do but also where we do it and how we go about getting it done. It also describes why it is we do it. This essay reflects and celebrates the special experience of being a community arts administrator. It is about people. It is about grassroots. And, it is about mountain wings.

––––––––

Being a community arts administrator means we do our best to help individuals learn to celebrate the cultural history of their community. In a way, it could be called "community arts restoration" because we help restore the rich, indigenous, cultural heritage of the community in which we work.

In the process, we help people rediscover their past and reclaim the vitality and creative expression of those persons who brought their community into being. It helps them to celebrate this cultural legacy in the context in which it was first created, helping them understand where they came from and how they got where they are as a community. This develops a special sense of pride for the cultural heritage and history that is uniquely theirs. In the process, we help them conserve, identify, celebrate, and transmit their unique community cultural values.

By bringing in and presenting outside arts experiences and diverse cultural expressions, we help them share in and appreciate the cultural heritage and history of other communities. This connects them with the larger human community through the one form of communication that transcends the barriers of society, the universal language - art. In this process of celebrating this history through art, these other communities can become a part of our lives as new seeds of old stories are planted. This is the gift of grounding - it is the gift of grassroots.

———

As community arts administrators, we encourage individuals to discover their own creativeness, giving them the opportunity to express themselves and celebrate the art of and in their lives. It opens them to new possibilities of who they are and, in turn, who they might become. This challenges them to become the best they can be.

This involves us not only in the work of arts education (protecting and encouraging the precious gift of imagination in children before it gets squeezed out of them), but also in "arts re-education," helping adults unlearn the misconceptions of art they acquired at an early age. In the process, we try to undo the damage done to them when they were young and named "uncreative" and/or art was named a product only "trained, paid-professionals do." We help people overcome their self-limitations as well as those placed on them by others who don't believe that people who participate in community arts activities, especially in rural and small communities, can be creative and produce professional quality arts experiences. We know the issue isn't quality, it's access, because we know that you can't have quality if you don't first have opportunity. And, we are about the business of creating and providing the opportunity which can, and quite frequently does, produce quality, in every sense of the word. It is a quality and excellence that is connected to the context of the community in which it is created. This is an indirect benefit of the community arts experience, and it puts us in the role of serving as a mentor.

We also know that presenting "quality, professional art" from outside the community context can be a wonderful teaching tool, inspiring and teaching all of us. It also contributes to our community creating a new vision of itself. So, we try to create the balance that brings the best of both of these together - process and product, art from the community and art presented to the community, recognizing the gifts of the community we serve. This also helps us protect the community authenticity and self-determination.

Everything we do is aimed at helping people understand the role of the arts in their lives and how the arts can be integrated into the fabric of everyday experience. We know that the way we go about doing this is as important as what it is that we are doing. Everything - from volunteer committee work, to presenting outside performances, to participating in community arts productions - is based on the commitment that the quality of the process is just as, if not more than, important as the quality of the product. When we forget this, we run the risk of contributing to our art becoming a commodity, a product, and the people with whom we work, little more than a means to an end - producing that product. If this happens, we also run the risk of becoming little more than merchants in art, perpetuating the approach to art that has alienated so many people from art in the first place by separating it out from our everyday lives. We know that community arts is not just about "bringing art to the people" - it is also about "bringing out the art in people" and we know the size of the community in no way limits the potential for this quality arts experience to occur.

This means that we challenge them, expecting the best they have to offer, demanding more than they think they have to give, believing in their creative ability - sometimes even more than they believe in it themselves. In the process, we nurture one of our greatest natural resources - our "rural genius." This is the gift of soaring - it is the gift of mountain wings.

As community arts administrators, we perform a kind of ministry. Not in the traditional use of the word, but rather in the sense of the root meaning of the word *administer* (ad + ministrare) which means "to serve." This is what we do - we serve the needs of those with whom we work by providing opportunities for a diverse community of people to gather together for a common purpose, sharing in the fellowship of the community arts experience. This gives them reason to see beyond the artificial barriers - to break through the walls separating them from each other - giving them something to celebrate and enjoy as one. It means helping them to work together and discover their lives can make a difference and what they do and they way they do it can indeed be quality, in the best sense of what the word means. It is a way of acknowledging that the people with whom we work are not a means to an end - a project or performance - but an end in and of themselves. They are the reason we do what we do. In the process, we help them create a new dialogue, a new way to talk about themselves and their community. This engages them in the exciting adventure of creating and developing a new vision for their lives and their community. It brings into existence a new spirit of working together to make that vision a reality. In the process, we help them learn to celebrate the diversity of who they are as individuals while, at the same time, inspiring a "sense of community" that enables them to share as one. This is the fellowship of grassroots and mountain wings - and as community arts administrators, we "minister" to this community spirit through the arts.

———

Being a community arts administrator means we must recognize that almost everything we do is political - or at least has political ramifications. The smaller the community, the more true this seems to be. This isn't just politics in the traditional sense of political parties and elections, but the politics of people and power, the hidden politics of those who really make decisions but are rarely ever seen. We learn that community arts, when it is successful, involves us in this political process, and it is part and parcel to everything we do. We learn to respect it and use it just like everyone else, only we try to use it better. We also try not to abuse it because we are committed to the concept of cultural democracy - the ideal that every person has the right to self-expression and that the story belongs to everyone. No one should be denied access to the story or to the telling of the story.

One of the things we learn is we can't accomplish this without working within the system. We also know that participating in the community arts experience can encourage individuals to take responsibility for their own lives resulting in a new sense of self-determination for their own future and sometimes even for the future of their community. The arts nurture leaders by nurturing the leadership qualities of expression and authentic voice. The arts challenge people to try something new, to go beyond what they know. The arts challenge people to do a little creative dreamthinking. As a result, the arts also prepare people to be better risk takers and sometimes this results in failure - but that is ok. We know that there can be valuable learning in failure and that one of the gifts of the community arts experience is that it provides a "learning ground" where people, individuals and groups, can engage in new things and be supported and nurtured regardless of the outcome. The community is a laboratory where we are allowed to experiment, even fail sometimes, in order to discover what it means to be fully human.

The other thing we come to realize is that the process just described can get us into trouble. It gets us into trouble because it is an indirect form of community organizing and the more individuals become involved in learning to express themselves and gain self-confidence and a positive self-image, the less likely they are to continue to let others make decisions for them. The more individuals risk change in their personal lives, the more likely they are to be open to change in other facets of their lives and the more willing they will be to accept ownership for what happens. This encourages them to become involved and not be willing to settle for others "doing it for them" anymore. Thus, we are about the business of creating opportunities for leaders to be developed, and this makes a significant contribution to the overall development of a community of which we are an important part.

So we realize that being a community arts administrator means we had better understand politics and power, and that we had better be risk-takers ourselves because we can't get others to take risks if we aren't willing to take them ourselves. And sometimes, when we do get into trouble, we need to be reminded that it may not be because we are doing a bad job - it just may well be because we are doing a good job. This is the challenge of being a community arts administrator - it is also the politics and paradox of grassroots and mountain wings.

––––––––

As community arts administrators, we know that marketing our program doesn't happen with newspaper ads, or slick brochures, or even subscription series campaigns. Marketing happens at the 10:00 a.m. coffee klatch, the women's club meeting, and on the volleyball court or at the young adult night-league in the high school gym. We know that it is the one-to-one communication, the "word-of-mouth marketing" that makes or breaks our program. So everything we do is involved in telling people what we are doing and why we are doing it. We are always telling those around us why the arts in our community are important. We are up against rigid barriers - preconceived notions of what the role of art is - and we know this will not be easy to change. But we have to try.

In a sense, we are storytellers, telling the stories of our community through the arts. We also tell the story of community arts. We tell it to the children and to their parents. We tell it to the Kiwanis and the Rotary clubs and the PTA. We tell it to the city and county government and to the state legislators and to anyone else who will listen, because not enough people have heard the story. And, unfortunately, many of those who have heard the story don't understand what it means.

And all the while we are telling the story, we know that people learn by doing, and the best way to help them understand the story is to participate in the story themselves. So, we are always extending an invitation to persons who never dreamed of becoming involved in the arts. And, sometimes they say yes, setting in motion a chain reaction that brings about change, enormous change. Change for the individual and, many times, unexpected change for the community. This is the unique responsibility of telling the story of grassroots and mountain wings and though we sometimes forget, storytelling is an art.

One of the things we know about being a community arts administrator is the pay isn't very good. We know we could make more money working somewhere else. But we work for less because we are driven by our missionary zeal, cursed with the passion of purpose. We also know it won't be done unless we do it (or, at least, we think it won't). And perhaps, because we are idealistic enough to believe that our lives and the lives of those around us can make a difference.

We also know that being a community arts administrator means that the people with whom we work, the volunteers and our board members, are many times our friends, our social circle because we share a common interest - the arts. And, it is difficult for many of them to distinguish between our public life and our private life. This, combined with the fact that in many communities (in particular, the small ones) being a community arts administrator puts us in a very visible, public position with the result that we are "on" almost everywhere we go. People lose us in our work and easily forget that we have a private life and there aren't that many who really understand what it is we do or why we do it anyway. This contributes to a real sense of isolation - of feeling out there by ourselves. And this can get very lonely.

Sometimes, this leads to depression and self-doubt - usually when we are the most tired, right after a major project that has occupied every moment of our life is over, and we realize we don't have the support group we need to share this with because we haven't been taking care of ourselves the way we should. The fact is, most of us are better care givers than care takers, and we pay the price for this. Sometimes we feel we just can't take it another day because of the endless committee meetings or the struggles with the board and/or the community politics. We are tired of always being a teacher and not being able to be a student. We go to conferences and workshops where hardly anyone running them understands how to translate their knowledge and resources into the context of rural and small communities - and we get tired of having to do this ourselves. We get frustrated at making it possible for everyone else to do their art but not having the time or energy to do our own. And, we get upset because those outside our community continue to make decisions affecting our work and our community because they have the power and the money to do so. What they don't always necessarily have is the same understanding we have about our community and the community arts development process. At times like this, it is easy to convince ourselves we haven't done a thing that makes a difference, and we suffer from all of the self-doubt and negative self-image possible. And we decide that our parents are right after all - maybe we should get a job that they can explain to their friends.

But it doesn't last long. Maybe we see someone who has changed because of our work. Or, we begin to see signs that some of the seeds we have sown are taking root and beginning to grow. Or perhaps we hear someone else tell the story of community arts, and we know they first learned that story from us. Or maybe we attend a meeting and make contact with other community arts administrators who speak the same language and share the same vision. And when this happens, we realize we aren't the only ones who feel this way or experience what we experience. We realize that we may be alone but we can stand being alone as long as we have company. And we finally get in touch again with the reason why we do what we do, and we become renewed and revitalized. We also realize that though we are held captive by the vision of grassroots and mountain wings, we are helplessly committed to this work. We also know that deep down inside us we wouldn't want it any other way.

Finally, we gain enough objectivity to realize that our lives are making a difference because we are helping people discover their cultural wealth, and, in the process, participate in bringing about positive change and growth in their individual lives and the life of the community in which they live. And this is special. What is even more special is that we begin to realize that it isn't "their" community more, it has become "our" community - and this is their gift to us. We learn that of all the gifts of grassroots and mountain wings, this is the most special - community arts has become our own touchstone to the human community.

We are community arts administrators. This is who we are. This is what we do. This is why we do it. This is our front porch.

The Deep Voice

The Relationship Between Art, Spirituality, and Healing

In 1994, PBS broadcast a program entitled "After Goodbye." It was a documentary focusing on the Turtle Creek Chorale, an internationally acclaimed male chorus. The program was about the loss and pain this organization had experienced since 1980, because over sixty of its members had died from complications associated with AIDS. It could have been a wrenching story, focusing only on the suffering and the devastation of personal and professional loss. It wasn't. The Emmy Award winning documentary eloquently portrayed how their art had become a source of strength, how their music had become a testament to the power of art to heal the human spirit. It was about the Chorale as a community of hope determined to triumph in the face of despair.

I had just serendipitously turned to the PBS station and happened to catch the very end of the program. Dr. Tim Seelig, Artistic Director of the organization, was concluding his eulogy for Randy Rhe, a much-loved member of the Chorale who died before the documentary was finished. Dr. Seelig closed his remarks by reading a poem that Randy had sent him a week before he died. The poem had no title and the author was not identified. It was a short, simple statement that Dr. Seelig believed spoke to what Randy Rhe and the Turtle Creek Chorale believed.

> *When you walk to the edge of all the light you have*
> *And take that first step into the darkness of the unknown,*
> *You must believe one of two things will happen:*
>
> *There will be something solid for you to stand upon,*
> *or, you will be taught how to fly.*

This documentary was not just about the Turtle Creek Chorale and their incredible strength and courage - it was about the power of art to transcend and transform the human condition. It was about the mystery of art and the way it can become the deep voice that heals the wounded heart and lifts the human spirit. It was about how art has a life of its own and weaves its own journey in and through our lives. I know this all to be true. I know because when I heard the poem Dr. Seelig read, I knew the title - it is called "Faith." I wrote it twenty-five years ago.

The arts aren't the cause of the crisis facing our culture, they are a cure. The arts aren't the source of the hurting in our society, they are a way of healing the pain. The arts are not in and of themselves, evil; they are an authentic expression of self that manifests an individual's courage to face life as it really is. Art that is not an authentic expression of self is not art - it is propaganda, or a product - but it is not art. Art is the voice of the soul struggling to express what it means to be human. Good and bad. When this voice is silenced, we lose an essential spiritual touchstone for what it means to be human.

For the past ten years we have listened to individuals accuse the arts and artists of being evil and those of us who participate in the arts are evildoers. We have been accused of obscenity, branded as pornographers. We have had almost every nasty, vile statement possible thrown in our face, but I have heard few voices stand up and challenge these charges. We have heard lots of indignation and anger from members of the arts community. But what we haven't heard are the clear, concise arguments that challenge these accusations. It is time for us to tell our story.

The arts are not evil. The arts are incapable of being evil in and of themselves. Art may be a voice that communicates about what evil is or might be, but it is not evil itself. To give art this kind of power is to change it from symbol to sign. This is the idolatry that is the true source of evil - making art an icon; so powerful it becomes the very thing it is communicating. People in the evangelical and political religious right do not have all the answers. I have known artists who are more spiritual in their work - even work that some consider to be nihilist and destructive - than some people who claim to be devoutly religious. Art expresses the truth - someone's truth - whether we like that truth or not. But I also know that just because art expresses truth doesn't mean it represents everyone's truth. And I have experienced people in the arts community being just as inflexible and intolerant as they claim the "other side" is being. The point isn't whether or not we accept each other's truth. The point is that we accept everyone's right to their own truth. What we must do, is recognize art as an authentic expression of what someone feels, thinks, or believes. If we don't, then we are missing the point of what art is all about. Art is the deep voice, nothing more, nothing less.

Sometimes the agonized vision of an artist trying to capture what is wrong with the world can be a powerful source of religious and spiritual insight. Sometimes, the only way we can learn and grow as a society is to be forced to face what it is we do not like. We thrive on denial, we don't like facing the truth. And artists are, if nothing else, truth-tellers. We may not like the truth they tell. We may not agree with the truth they portray, but it is, to them, truth. It is their authentic voice. And many times it is a courageous voice, because it is not always popular to be a truth-teller. Sometimes, what appears to be one thing really can be something altogether different. This is the confusing aspect of creative expression - it is one of the great paradoxes of metaphor.

Despite what some people think, the debate surrounding the arts and their role in our society isn't just a national debate focusing on the NEA and public funding for art. These issues are just as relevant for people who live in rural and small communities and are becoming more so each day. In 1990, I was asked to testify on behalf of the NEA to the House Sub-Committee on Appropriations. That was the year when the Mapplethorpe and Serrano controversies had dominated the hearings. Speaking on behalf of the arts in rural and small communities, I said the following:

> *For people in rural and small communities, art is not past tense, something that has already happened - an event or a thing. Art is present tense, a verb that excites, challenges, demands, changes, reveals, angers, threatens, and encourages. And yes, it is something that sometimes causes outrage and indignation. But art has always done that. For art has always been the voice of the soul and sometimes the soul for which it speaks is in pain. We may want to turn our heads when it becomes uncomfortable or threatening, but to do so is to deny that not all is right with the world. If art is the voice of the soul then it is a voice that cannot lie. From the words of the poet in Psalm 130 "out of the depths I cry unto thee O God," which laments the poet's feeling of being alone and perhaps even deserted by God; to the canvas of Picasso called Guernica which expresses his outrage of the terror-bombing of Guernica during the Spanish Civil War in 1937; to the unsettling photographic images of Robert Mapplethorpe which cry out with all of the anger and outrage of a wounded soul who cannot find peace in a world that*

refuses to accept who he is, the voice cannot lie. It sometimes speaks of desertion, of being alone, of being angry, because it is. It is sometimes the voice of indignation and protest when the world is unfair because no other voice has the integrity and the courage to do so. I am outraged there are those who believe we have a right to control and/or silence these voices. What I find obscene is that in the midst of all the controversy, I have heard no one discuss Mapplethorpe, the man, his outrage, or the pain his images were intended to invoke. And I am disappointed that the controversy has obscured the beauty and brilliance of the work displayed in the exhibition.

Of the twenty-four witnesses, there were few who defended the work of Mapplethorpe. I was surprised and disappointed. For many people in the arts community, Mapplethorpe was a trouble maker and didn't represent what the rest of us were doing. The problem is, we can't defend our right to freedom of expression without granting him the same. We are all in this together.

I was also surprised and disappointed that most religious denominations chose to be silent on this issue. Contrary to what many people think, there are a lot of ministers and members of congregations who agree with what I said. There is a long tradition in Christianity of understanding the role of art as the authentic voice of the soul and an expression of the human condition. This is not to say that all of Christianity broadly embraces the role of art. It doesn't. And I wish the church had been more willing to take a stand in support of the arts. But it didn't do that either. This does not change the fact that there are many people who are deeply religious and believe in the role of art as an expression of the human spirit.

Unfortunately, my experience has been the arts community itself is just as capable of being prejudiced and intolerant as is any other group. There is a tendency by some people involved in the arts to stereotype anyone associated with the Christian faith or any formal religious tradition as an evangelical, religious and political zealot who goes around branding everyone involved in the arts as idolaters and demons. The fact is, any prejudice, regardless of its target, is destructive and contrary to community-making. I know the evangelical religious and political right does not have a corner on God. I also know that those involved in the arts do not have a corner on truth either. Most of us in our society find ourselves caught in the middle between these polarized extremes. We have been pointing a lot of fingers at each other. What we haven't been doing very well is extending each other the common courtesy of listening to each other.

I think many people have missed an essential point - the National Endowment for the Arts (NEA) and other public funding agencies do not make art, they help make art happen. Funding support is an invitation to an artist and arts organizations to engage in the creative process, supporting those who make art happen. To control what is done once this process begins would be to violate the freedom of expression of the artist. To do so would be to violate self-determination and authenticity of what is created. The easy thing to do would be to stop all public funding for the arts altogether. And there have been many trying to make this very thing happen. But this doesn't solve the problem. And how tragic this would be - to deny the opportunity for even a little amount of our tax dollars to be used in all of the wonderful, creative, community-making ways I have discussed in this book, because a few people don't like what another few people are creating. How wrong it would be to take away such a small, insignificant amount of our federal budget with which we have been able to do so much. How wrong-headed to believe that federal funding is the problem.

Funding for the arts isn't the problem, it is our failure to understand the role of the arts that is the problem. Yes, public support for the arts is wrought with risk. But that is what art is about - risk. Risking new things, risking boundaries being challenged, and risking being outraged. By its very nature, art provokes - that is what it is supposed to do - provoke our senses, provoke us into feeling, into experiencing something. Anything. When we only look at art as a noun - something that can be defined as good or bad, right or wrong - we objectify it. In the process, we remove it from the realm of everyday life of people. This makes art powerless to affect lives in a positive way because it takes art out of the context in which it was created. In the final analysis, art isn't objects, it isn't performances, it isn't products - it is the deep voice. And, as the deep voice, it can and will not lie. The arts aren't the cause of our social crises, they are a cure.

It is time for those of us involved in the arts to speak up and speak out. We need to do so with a loud voice full of every ounce of conviction we have. It is time we talk about the relationship between art and spirituality and art and healing. We have evidence of this relationship - it is verifiable. We know it personally and we know it as communities. Organizations like the Turtle Creek Chorale know it too. They learned it in their individual lives as artists. They experienced it together as they began to make a community of art. They created a community of healing as they shared their art with others. This is the truth that thousands of arts organizations, artists, and audiences all across our country know. The arts are spiritual. The arts heal. This is one of the core values driving our work in community arts development. It has been this way from the beginning.

We cannot continue to let others communicate our values, misrepresenting what it is we do and why we are doing it. That is why we are in the difficulty we are in now. We have been outraged and we have been angry. We have done a good job of communicating this. What we haven't done is effectively communicate why it is we are upset. We have not been telling people what it is we believe. More importantly, we have not been telling people why it is we believe this.

What are these values we need to communicate? Well, a value is defined as a basic orientation to the world around us - that is, a world view. For many of us involved in the community arts development, we believe the arts are deeply connected to the human spirit. The arts are the deep voice. This is where the arts connect with spirituality. I use the word spirituality because people tend to confuse religion and spirituality. Religion is associated more with an institution, an existing belief system that has its structures and rituals to perpetuate its existence. Spirituality, on the other hand, has a much more individual sense to it, focusing on the individual journey. It is much more of a process in which people engage rather than a particular way or place in which they do this engaging. Closely connected to this concept is the belief that art is also involved in the process of healing. Let me explore these two core values in the remainder of this essay.

Art and Spirituality

A few years ago I attended a workshop that was presented by Sam Keene, a colleague of Joseph Campbell. During the workshop on health and wholeness, he made a statement that was so simple it was breathtaking. He pointed out that we have never been able to make a distinction between sensuality and sexuality in our society. We probably owe much of this confusion to the Puritans who brought their strict religious view of the world with them to their new existence. Without question, this fear of art as the source of temptation and evil has been a core value driving the development of our nation from the beginning, especially in our rural and small communities. It was the turn of the century before theatre was even allowed in most rural communities because it was viewed as being a source of evil. It took the Tent Chautauqua (using the name Chautauqua to appear to be certified by the Church), to bring about a slow, deliberate change to this attitude. Many people in rural and small communities are still suspicious of the arts because of this strong historical tradition. This is exactly one of the reasons this current controversy over public funding for the arts is so closely connected to our rural and small communities.

Well, the arts are sensuous - by their very definition the arts appeal to the senses. You can't have art without sensuality - it's not possible. This is the very definition of aesthetics - to feel, to experience. And the way we do this is through the senses. This is part of the gift the arts give to all of us - the inspiration to feel and to experience the world around us, in all of its glory and all of its shadow-side.

The Ascending and Descending Role of Art

A few years ago I was asked to participate in a think-tank meeting for the Theatre Program at the NEA. This meeting was held at the height of the threat to defund the NEA. Needless to say, the conversation in the room was intense because everything we believed in was under attack, including the NEA itself. There were two people who were constantly arguing back and forth with each other. It was obvious to the rest of us they had a shared history and what was going on was a continuation of something started long before they came into the room that morning. They knew each other and they knew what each believed. So much so, it seemed impossible for them to listen to each other. They had developed a code between them, and most of us really didn't understand what was going on.

One, from a very prestigious private foundation, kept talking about the beauty and magnificence of art because it lifted her spirit. To her, art makes meaning and beauty and this is the kind of art her foundation was interested in funding. This is art that inspires transcendence. The other person was from a theatre company from the south and he talked about art as that which must challenge the status-quo. To him, art is not something created to be beautiful, or to make people pleasant or happy or comfortable. Art is something that confronts what is wrong and unjust in our society and is designed to make people feel uncomfortable. To him, art reveals what is wrong with our world and, in so doing, demands something be done to change it. This is art that inspires transformation.

As I listened to them, it seemed to me they weren't really disagreeing. In essence, they were both saying the same thing, but in a different way. To understand the nature of art, we have to understand it in both its "ascendant" and "descendent" purpose. Art can, through ascendance, through the elevation of the human spirit, help us transcend what we know, what we see, what we understand. When art does this it is "awful" (that is, full of awe). This is when art lifts the spirit. It is the exhale - art that empties us and sucks the air out of our lungs because of its power and the truth of the simple/complexity it portrays in such a profound way. This is when art reveals mystery and truth and grasps us with such intensity that it transcends the human condition, and leaves us changed, forever. Art is one of the few things left in our world that can create this much-needed sense of "awe-fullness" in us.

But there is another function of art, art as descendence. Art can be an invitation (sometimes compelling) to descend from the surface of our lives - beyond the facade and the masks, to the depths of our existence - the deep place where truth exists. When art does this, it is the inhale - driving us into ourselves, forcing us to gasp for air, taking in the force and intensity of the experience inside of us because of the power and the truth of the simple/complexity it portrays in such a powerful way.

The one, the descendent function, reveals what is and shouldn't be. The other, the ascendant function, reveals what isn't but could be. Art can be beautiful and lift our spirits - but art can also force us to face the truth - to descend to the deep place and see the world as it is and shouldn't be. They both do the same thing - they are a way we can transcend the condition of our lives - a way we are transformed. These two functions cannot be separated - they are converse images of the same creative force - the same truth.

This is the truth that I have come to know in my life. I have experienced it on a personal basis and I have witnessed it in the lives of people with whom I have lived and worked. When art fulfills the ascendant function, it connects with the human spirit in such a way as to help us transcend the limits of our humanity. When art fulfills the descendent function, it confronts us with the hurt and wounds of a world of injustice and oppression. It connects us with the human spirit in such a way as to transcend the hurt and invite us to healing. They are both essential parts of the human experience and the arts are intimately connected to both experiences. The relationship between art and spirituality is not new, but it is something we have seriously neglected.

If there is anything we have not done a good job of, it is understanding the critical importance of the relationship between the ascendant and descendent function of art. This should be one of the most important conversations we have. This should be the content of the discourse we have with one another. Not just with those of us who support the arts, but with those who think the arts are the cause of our social problems. We aren't ever going to bring an end to the religious and cultural war dividing this nation until we can sit down and talk with each other. And that means we have to quit pointing our fingers at each other and blaming the other side for everything that is wrong. We are past the point of blame - it doesn't matter anymore who is at fault or who caused the problem. The fact is, there are problems facing our society and our communities and we are spending all of our time placing blame rather than using our creative imaginations to work together to find the solution.

What we must be clear about are our values. If we believe art is related to spirituality, we shouldn't be embarrassed or afraid to say so. If we believe art is connected to healing, we shouldn't hold back. Tell people and tell them why. If we tell them why we will probably do it by telling them a story. It will be a story about our life and the role art has played in helping heal our wounds, or celebrating our joy. Or we will be telling the story about someone else's life, where the same thing happened. Perhaps we won't change anything in telling the story to someone who thinks or believes differently than we do, but we will have accomplished one thing - we will have moved the discussion from confrontation to conversation. Better yet - don't tell them, show them. Let them see this truth through the art we do and the way we do it. The worst thing that can happen is they won't listen to us, and that already happens. But at least we will begin to experience each other as individuals. My experience with the arts community is that it consists of some of the most caring and loving people I have ever met. This is certainly true for those involved in community arts development in rural and small communities. We need to celebrate this aspect of who we are and do a better job of telling those around us.

The power of the arts to transcend and transform the human condition comes because the arts create circles of convergence, a place for people to meet and to share and to talk and to listen. The arts invite relationship. This is the reason the arts are one of the very positive and creative ways we can rebuild the front porch of America - the arts help create and celebrate the community spirit that is essential for any community to survive.

Art and Healing

One of the very important things the arts do is to invite healing. This is one of the aspects that needs to be identified in the relationship between art and spirituality. There are many people in many different community situations who are beginning to realize the important role the arts play in this arena of human healing. The best way I know to talk about this and the effect it can have on people's lives is to share a personal experience.

In 1994, our country spent a lot of time and energy celebrating the 50th anniversary of the end of World War II. Something happened to me during this celebration that helped me understand better what it is I believe about the power of art to heal.

I currently serve a small rural congregation as a bi-vocational minister (part-time). It is in the community of Huntsville, Missouri, a small community consisting of less than 1,500 people. With the closing of the mine and the railroad cutbacks, it is a community that is in great pain.

In April of 1994, a member of my church, Neil Block, who is my age and is a Vietnam veteran, approached me with a request. The local chapter of the VFW (Veterans of Foreign Wars) wanted me to speak at the dedication of the Huntsville Vietnam Memorial. I am a Vietnam veteran as well, and I have not spoken about my experience overseas since 1968, when I returned. My first response to Neil was an immediate "Oh, no. I don't think I could do that." That response had nothing to do with my being a minister, or a person trained as a speaker. That response was based on my being a veteran and not thinking I could do an effective job of talking about the war. As I thought about the invitation, I decided perhaps it was time for me to talk about the War and my experience, and the impact it had on me and my generation. I reluctantly said yes but I made it clear that I would be speaking as a veteran, not as a minister. The VFW agreed. What happened as a result of this decision had a tremendous impact on my life, and perhaps the lives of some of the citizens in the Huntsville community as well. The speech was delivered on Memorial Day.

The Healing Wall

The community gathered together in front of the memorial - a small stone seat that had the names of those who died in Vietnam inscribed on it. The decision to establish this memorial was the result of the Vietnam Memorial Moving Wall that had found its way to the community of Huntsville.

During the speech on that Memorial Day, I spoke to a large crowd consisting of an unusual mix of older and younger people. During the speech, I shared my experiences in Vietnam. First, for a brief time, I served on the USS Providence, a flagship stationed in the Gulf of Tonkin. I was on staff of the Commander Seventh Fleet. As a communications yeoman, part of my job was to monitor all communications from the combat zone and re-code it for transmission to the United States. I spent hours at the teletype, reading casualty reports - graphic descriptions of the wounds and/or manner of death of U.S. soldiers in the war - and then transmitting those reports back to the states. I spent my entire time on that ship dealing with the war and with death.

The second experience I shared was when the ship I was on entered Danang Harbor early one morning to provide ground support fire. We had a captain of the flag ship who believed we should be a fighting flag ship, so we left the Gulf of Tonkin, headed toward the harbor, arriving before dawn. I was told that first night, when I was on watch, that I should go outside and observe if I could. We had five and six inch mounts on the front of the cruiser and we were to fire them to provide ground support fire for cover and troop advancement. And so when I got off watch, I put on my flak jacket and went out on the top deck of the ship, right behind the six inch mounts. I filled my ears with cotton and waited for the guns to fire. It was a powerful experience, an overwhelming sight. I stood there absolutely mesmerized by the recoil burst of flame - the July Fourth envy of any place but there. But then, after a long time being hypnotized by the power of that powder blast, I happened to look in the direction of where the shells were fired. At that moment I caught a glimpse of the hillside where one of the shells exploded. I don't know how many died in that explosion. I didn't know who I was part of killing, but I knew. I stood there, sick to my stomach, sick at heart. There are few times when an individual can point to one moment in time and say, "this is where I lost my innocence, this is where I was changed, forever." I can. I have never been able to forget that moment.

My final experience was two months prior to returning to the States for my discharge from the service. I was temporarily stationed at the US Naval Hospital in Yokouska, Japan, where they brought the air-vacs (the battle wounded) from Nam for hospital care before their return to the states. My job was to interview those people when they first came to the hospital and get the necessary information for preparation to send them home. I will never forget the devastation I saw - the physical destruction and damage done to vital, young, men who would never be the same. Eighteen and nineteen-year-olds who had lost arms, or legs, or half their faces to a mine. Pieces of human beings, some hardly intact enough to be considered alive, let alone live a normal or productive life. Of all the things I experienced when I was overseas, I think that has left the greatest mark of all, the deepest wound. And as difficult as all of that was, I was fully aware that I had been spared the horror and the trauma of the face to face battle our soldiers had to experience in the fields and marshes of Vietnam. I had been one of the lucky ones.

After I shared these experiences, I closed my speech with a poem I wrote specifically for the dedication ceremony. It was a poem that had been stored up in me ever since I saw the Vietnam Memorial in Washington several years before. The invitation to speak about the Vietnam Memorial in Huntsville resulted in my using my own art to discuss the Vietnam Memorial in Washington D.C. As I read the poem, I experienced first hand, not only the healing my art can give to others but also the healing that I could experience myself through someone else's art as well as the art I created about this experience to share with others. I share this poem to celebrate this power of art to heal.

The Healing Wall

I ignored the Wall -
for a long time
I had managed to keep out unwanted reminders
of the memories of what I saw and did and felt
and the Wall threatened to violate this self-truce.
For a while, I refused to go to the Wall.
I came close, but could not bring myself to go down
into that black hole -
So I stood there alone, on the perimeter
of the large descending block of black, cold stone,
and watched from my vantage point on the hill above.

Concealed by the autumn shadows,
hands pocketed, I turned my back and walked away,
mumbling to myself in a voice so low
even I couldn't hear what I was saying,
"Not today, I cannot do this today."

II

I visited the Wall.
One evening in the late summer of the year,
when the cool winds blew across the Mall and the
early evening sun was crisp, I went to the Wall, again.
I stood where I had stood before but refused to go,
And without ever deciding,
without ever giving consent
I found myself moving toward it,
pulled by some force I could not see,
drawn by memories I could no longer deny.
I began the slow descent into the dark hole,
not wanting to but needing to go back into
what I had spent twenty-five years trying to forget.

At first tentative, I stood next to the first point of the Wall-
looking down the long descent of widening black granite,
wanting to turn back, but I had committed,
this time I needed to go.
I walked down the path, head down,
unable to look up at the Wall -
afraid I would see a name, recognize a name, any name.
Perhaps a name I had seen before, a death I knew before
his family knew. Perhaps a friend, someone who died and
I didn't know.

I couldn't look but I could feel its presence -
As I descended, it cast a silent, shadow, growing on me.
As the sun went down, the darkness deepened.
I stopped where the walk meets in the middle,
joining the two parts of the Wall together -
the deepest part of the Memorial
and slowly, my eyes began their climb up the Wall.
Groove by groove, name by name,
I saw what I knew would be there -
names - hundreds and thousands of names
carved into the cold hard flesh of that stone -
first names and last names
carved by the trauma and devastation of the bombs
and the mines and the sniper fire -
and the yells and the screams
of young men dying and not knowing why.
I heard the haunting sound of the death
of all of those soldiers whose
names I had seen and passed on to those places back
home who would receive the telegram
"We regret to inform you. . ."
I saw the names, blurred as they were,
I saw them and I could not move.

III

I touched the Wall - down in the deep hole where I stood,
I moved forward - not wanting to
but needing to feel it ,
needing to trace the edges of at least one name -
not to remember, but to forget.
I touched the smooth stone, gingerly at first, with one finger
feeling the contrast between that and the rough place, where the
stone had been violated by the name carved into it -
And, in the stillness of that moment

(I remember the stillness, particularly the stillness),

I did what all who go there must do,
I put my whole hand, palm down, against the stone -
first one hand and then the other, softly first,
Then pressing my palm harder against the Wall until
The full weight of my body leaned against it.
Braced by the stone, held up by its quiet, dignified, strength,
I became connected to the Wall,
connected to everything that happened, everything I had felt,
everything I had avoided for over twenty-five years.
Then I was no longer leaning against the Wall,
I was becoming part of the Wall, or the Wall part of me.
The more I tried to pull away, the more I couldn't move.
It began to pull out of me
emotions I had not felt since I was there,
since that first moment I saw and knew
I had been part of someone's death -
reliving the moment of lost innocence,
remembering the emptiness,
feeling again, the sickness in my heart
I had kept numb for years.
That is when the first tear came, and then a second,
followed by more -
slow tears, warm tears from down deep inside the hole of me.
I became a prisoner of the Wall, captive by its silent,
vigilant, roll call of death.

Then I began to move my hands over the Wall -
over names I did not know,
slow at first, and then faster, almost frantically -
at first not knowing why -
but then knowing -
I was looking for one name,
I was looking for the one groove my hands
would know the best,
the one that would confirm what I always knew
to be true but was afraid to admit,
a name that wasn't there but should have been -
mine.

It was that sudden realization,
that revelation of surprise,
when it all rushed in,
when it all came back in on me - overwhelming me,
forcing me to face what I had not been able to face before,
the source of my guilt, my one great sin -
I had lived. I had come back home.

I was no more deserving than any one of these names,
but I survived.
My hands connected to the Wall,
I gave it back - and the Wall took it, all -
the hurt, the pain, the grief, the guilt, the shame.
For the very first time since coming home -
I cried about the War.

These were not slow tears,
they were fast, they were hot and they burned.
I wept for me and I wept for every single family
and town those names, those grooves, touched.
I leaned against that Wall and
it held me up
and I finally let go.

When I was empty, out of tears,
the Wall let go and I pulled away.
I looked around and saw others who had done or
were doing the same as I had done.
Each of us in our own way, letting go.
We looked at each other - we didn't speak, but we knew
and shared, in silence.
It was there, beyond the Wall,
I began to heal.

IV

I left the Wall
I ascended from that deep hole.
Tired, emotionally exhausted,
I looked back where I had been.
I knew my pain had not magically left me -
I carry it with me today -
but I carry it, it no longer carries me.
This was the healing I could not find before -
The Wall told me my name was not there
and said "Go live your life, you do not belong here."
And so I do, live my life now, beyond the Wall.

As I turned to walk away,
I overheard a small boy,
 unaware of war and all its tragedy,
ask his father - "Why are there so many names
on the wall, Daddy?"
and his father's soft reply echoes in my heart, even now-
because I knew he too knew the Wall
the way I knew the Wall -
he replied with the only answer any of us
who have been there have to give -
"I do not know. I do not know."

Epilogue

*To this day I do not know why
we have carved so many names on so many walls,
but we have.
But what I also know is there are many casualties of war
we never see carved on walls -
deaths not recorded by grooves chiseled in stone -
kept secret, even from those of us who need to know
the most.
So, as we gather together at this
and all the other walls of war in the world,
let us also honor those of us who lived
with a silent, vigilant, prayer -
a prayer ever present on our lips
and in our hearts. . .*

No more walls, please, no more walls.

I will never forget that afternoon in Huntsville. It was an emotional experience for all of us. Following my speech, people were very quiet, still. It reminded me of my visit to the Wall in D.C. Slowly, people began to move, looking through the crowd for someone to hold, to hug. There was a need to touch. There was not a lot of talking. I saw men of my father's generation with tears running down their faces, something that is all too rare for them. I saw sons and fathers embrace - with a kind of knowing and understanding that may not have existed before. That afternoon in May invited a small community, deeply wounded by the war, to heal. My speech and poetry did not do the healing. The people did. What I did was extend the invitation. What writing the poem did was invite me to name my own healing and celebrate it. And, by sharing the poem with that community, I invited others to name their own healing and celebrate it with each other as well.

I have shared this with you for two reasons. The first is to acknowledge that I know the healing power of art. Art is a healing wall. I have experienced it on a personal basis - as a person who visited a work of art, a memorial, and felt the power of art as symbol reach inside and heal a deep wound. I have also experienced it on a professional basis, as an artist. I have watched it in the eyes of those who hear and recognize the name of what I write and what I say - realize the power of the metaphor and take it for themselves.

That day in Huntsville was a day that began a healing process in the hearts and minds of many of those who shared that experience with each other. I have seen it happen in communities of all sizes. This is how the healing power of art becomes part of the rebuilding of the front porch of America. It happens every day at the Vietnam Memorial in Washington D.C. It happened in Huntsville. It begins when someone discovers their own voice by making art. It continues when someone shares their voice with others and risks the unknown. And it reaches its fullest community-making potential when people find a way to share their stories with each other - their discoveries, their pain and struggle, the triumph and tragedy of their lives. When they do this, art becomes their healing wall.

Art transcends. Art transforms. Art is the deep voice that heals the wounded heart and lifts the human spirit.

Metaphor - The Final Freedom

The poet is an inscape artist,
capturing on a canvas of words,
glimpses of the internal environment
encountered in the journey through self
in search of the soul.

When art is made personal, it has the power to transform. Art is a way into ourselves, discovering who we are, what we think, why we feel what we feel. It connects us with the deep self. It is a key that unlocks secrets of who we are and why we are this way. Art is one of the few ways we as human beings can put a name to those forces in our life that influence us, including those that can't be seen. It is the recognition that language is symbol and art is the most symbolic language of all. Art therapists, and others in psychology as well, long ago discovered the power of the creative, symbolic language of art as a way to reveal secrets and dreams.

Many of us in the arts also discovered long ago the healing power art has when we are able to create these symbols and name what was before unnameable. That is not to say the only value of the arts is as a psychological expression of individuals. Art is certainly more than this. But we need to recognize the importance of having this opportunity of self-expression available and what happens to us when we don't. Language is one of the ways we come into existence in the world. The problem with language is that as we learn it, we are at the same time, limited by it. We learn language by learning rules - rules of semantics (meaning) and rules of syntax (structure). The more we learn these rules the more effectively we are able to communicate. But, paradoxically, the more we learn and adhere to the rules, the more it limits our freedom of expression.

This is where art comes into the picture. Art is symbol language. But it is not a language that is limited or restricted by rules. Art breaks the rules. Sometimes, art helps bring new rules into existence. Art can be a kind of linguistic and symbolic liberation. It is the language of the creative imagination. As such, it has great power in our lives. It can also have great power in the lives of others who experience it in relationship to the artists and the art they create.

Art not only provides the opportunity to reveal who we are to ourselves and others, but who we want to be. And, in some mysterious way, the revealing of these "possibilities" actually can provide us with a way to become what it is that is revealed. It serves as a kind of creative self-fulfilling prophecy, a positive way to "practice" or "rehearse" ourselves into a new kind of existence. This especially occurs when the art we are practicing is our own. It can also happen when we practice the art that has been created by someone else. Theatre, music, dance, poetry - can all be symbols of someone else's self-expression and discovery. They are called arts disciplines - forms of expression that can be studied, learned, reproduced through the discipline of practice. As we practice the art of others, we can discipline ourselves into the performance/presentation of this art. To do this, we must make room for it in our lives. And when we make room for this, we are expanding the potential of who we are as individuals. We broaden our capacity to experience and feel in new ways. This is why theatre has so much to offer. It is storytelling that requires the ability to feel and experience the story to make it work. It forces us to become more than we are by ourselves, placing us in the shoes of someone else, making us "walk their talk." Participating in this type of experience can be a personally empowering experience for the artists and the audience alike.

The Alfred Arvolds, Baker Brownells, and Robert Gards of our world have known one more secret - the only thing more powerful than theatre that tells someone else's story, is theatre that is created by us to tell our own story. It gives us permission to acknowledge who we are. It also provides us with an invitation to be someone different than who we are. And accepting this invitation can give us the courage to act on that invitation. For some of us, it is the only escape we have from the confines of our existence, from the boundaries and rules imposed upon us. For some of us, it is the way we can communicate our hopes and our dreams. It is the power of the imagination - the ability to think of and/or create something other than the way things are. Or, perhaps, another way to think of it is that art is fantasy brought into the realm of reality through the power of our imagination. Whatever it is, art is the voice of the soul struggling to express what it means to be human.

And, when we find this voice, when we rehearse it and practice it, our imagination is engaged and perhaps even enlarged. As a result, we have the potential of experiencing something we know to be true. This is why I believe metaphor is the unconditional grace of our imagination. No right, no wrong. No internal judgements, no outside evaluation. Total freedom to explore, to experience. Freedom to discover the truth in what we see - the truth of what the world is and shouldn't be and the truth of what the world isn't, but could be.

This is the power of metaphor. This is why metaphor is the final freedom. When all else is taken from us - when we are stripped of our wealth, our position, our prestige - we still have the power of transcending that reality through metaphor. Metaphor allows us not only to transcend the condition of our lives, but in rare moments, actually end up transforming our lives. This is how art is connected to hope. Metaphor is a way that helps us act out the condition of our lives and, in the process, act our way out of this condition.

Metaphor doesn't change the world, it changes the way we look at it. It is, in the final analysis, the only thing we have that allows us to not be confined by the world around us. It is our escape - it is our entry - into the human condition. It is the magical incantation that opens the doors that were previously closed. It is the single most powerful and liberating aspect of being human. The capacity to create metaphor is one of the most powerful and exciting ways we have to be fully human.

Metaphor And Community-Making

There is another aspect of art that is important to understand. Art as story. Art is the invitation to tell our story and to listen to the story of others. When this happens, when art is made personal and then shared with those around us, it invites the creation of community. Perhaps the community it creates is only momentary, but it is nonetheless, authentic. And this community-making aspect of art is what sets it apart from almost any other kind of human experience. It opens up who we are to others and lets them see us, the real us, inside. It is an invitation to others not only to see who we are, but to experience us in relationship. There is a great risk involved in doing this because it makes us open and vulnerable to rejection. But, to not do this is to doom ourselves to social isolation, condemn ourselves to living in our separateness. This act of giving and of risking, is, in and of itself, an act of creative hope - hope that someone will hear what we are saying and understand what we are feeling. It is also hope that someone will share with us and identify with us and be like us. Perhaps even like us. At a minimum, we hope for respect that what it is we have shared will be cared for as an extension of us. It does not have to be liked, but it does have to be valued because it represents who we are. And we, as the audience, as the ones who receive this gift of sharing - be it song or picture, word or dance - we are also changed. We are transformed because we have shared in the experience of this sharing. When someone shares at the level of authentic expression, it is almost impossible to walk away unchanged, unaffected. Great art grasps us, takes hold of us in a powerful grip and shakes our sense of reality until it, and we, are no longer the same.

As I have worked with people and participated in helping them to discover their own creative expression, I have witnessed this authentic sharing, this personal and communal transformation. And the power of the personal transformation of the artist can be passed, like a torch, from the one who created it to the one who receives it. And that creative spark - that quantum leap over the orchestra pit or the surge of words off the page into our soul - enters our lives and takes on a personal power all its own. It is one of the great mysteries of life - this power of those who watch and witness to transcend and be transformed. I cannot explain it but I have experienced it on a personal level. I have experienced it as an artist, and I have experienced it as a member of an audience. I know it to be true.

The Long View

When I look at the generation of those young people between the ages of 20-35, what some call the 13th generation, I see a group of young people, many of whom believe the way of the world has already been set for them and they have no say in its outcome. I see it in the students who sit in my classroom. I listen to it as they talk about the world around them. No generation before has had so much thrown at them - information, conflict, fear, stress, uncertainty - on a daily basis. Many of them have surrendered already to the comfort of cynicism because it hurts too much to care. But the cynic is nothing more than a poet whose heart has hardened. They are poets too sensitive for the world, so they pretend they don't care. But, living their pretense is as powerful a metaphor as anything they see around them. And, as they practice this cynicism, as they rehearse it day by day, it becomes their reality. It is not a creative reality. It is not a reality that manifests much hope, but it is a reality all the same. What they do not have is the long view- it simply doesn't exist for them.

Some of them, especially those who are currently teenagers, have gone beyond cynicism - actually into the final stage beyond cynicism - fatalism. Cynicism is a negative feeling, but it is a feeling. Fatalism is a blind acceptance of things the way they are because of the belief they were meant to be this way. It is a way not to feel. It is an emotional numbness and this is the worst surrender of all. And they seek any "anesthetic" they can find to help deaden the feeling.

But the fact is, they do feel, they do care. This generation we call "X" has an enormous capacity to care. I see it in their own rituals and their own expressions. I don't think of them as Generation X - I think of them as Generation Y (why?). They are not totally negative, they are just incredibly realistic. And not all of them have given into the cynicism. I am always amazed when I listen to my students address problems. They are vibrant and full of energy. They are "crafty-wise" and creative. Some of them have taken clear stock of the situation and have already begun to address the future for their own lives. But it seems to be a defensive future - a future based on what they have already accepted as the way things will be. What seems to be lacking in many of them is the expression of hope that things can change. They don't know the transcending and transforming power of metaphor. There is a reason for this. They are the first generation that has grown up in a society that not only doesn't value art, it devalues it. We live in a society that has offered few of them the invitation to discover the unconditional grace of their imagination.

There are some people in our society disappointed in this younger generation. I'm not. I'm impressed they have done so well with what they have had thrown at them. I am disappointed in those of us who raised them - we have done them a great disservice. We have robbed some of them of their dreams because we have not helped them learn how to dream. We have given them too much information and not told them what to do with it (basically because we don't know ourselves). They learn too much too quickly, and they don't know what to do with what they know. Some of these young people have no imagination. We may be angry with them, but what we should be is scared for them - we must accept the fact we have left them little choice. What we have not done is take the long-view. We have been so busy experiencing the world ourselves and being concerned about our own needs being met, we have failed to address the future. Their future.

We have allowed many of our children to have everything done for them. Life, to them, is a constant feed through the cable wires - every picture presented to them through television and film.

We have left little to the imagination. They don't have to do anything. We have allowed them to be spectators. No, we have encouraged them to watch the world instead of participating in it. I see students in my classroom every day who have succumbed to this mentality. If it isn't spectacle, they get bored. It is as if they have to be entertained, because that is what we did with them instead of raising them, teaching them, nurturing them. They are disconnected because there was never any family or neighborhood or community for them to be connected to. Many of them have spent their entire life being overstimulated and under challenged.

There is an interesting tradition that exists in some Native American cultures. It is called the "Seventh Generation." It is used as a basis for making decisions, a kind of personal and tribal community evaluation document. The decisions they make are based on how that decision will affect the seventh generation that comes into existence after the decision is made. This is the long-view. We must start making decisions based on the seventh generation from now. And do our best to deal with what wasn't done seven generations ago.

Those of us in the arts are not guilt-free. We have been fighting so many political battles, so many social concerns, so many issues surrounding our own survival, we have sometimes taken the comfort of the short-view. We have been fighting for increased funding when we should have been fighting for our children and their children's children. Funding won't give our children the gift of metaphor. The arts will. And we can't keep expecting someone else to do this for us. We are going to have to find the way to do it ourselves. We have been struggling for our own survival when we should have been fighting for the survival of our communities. The world is too much with them and we have not protected them. We have been creating advocacy arguments rather than finding new ways to help our children and our communities learn the liberating and creative power of metaphor. Perhaps it is time for us to revisit the lesson ourselves.

Beyond Despair

What do we do to combat this cynicism, this fatalism? We have to focus our efforts on rebuilding the front porch. We have to find ways to stop the disintegration of the family that is devastating our society. We have to focus on being neighborhoods and communities again. We have to quit letting things happen without doing anything about it. We have to begin to act out and act on our hope for the future. One of the ways to do all of this is through the arts. Those of us involved in the arts need to make this a crusade - a social mandate to acquaint every human being with the unconditional grace of the imagination.

This crusade is not about making art available to those who can afford it. It is not about promoting art as noun - so people can attend more arts events. We must reclaim the concept of art as verb, art as action. Self-expression is the one inalienable right that can not be taken away from us - the freedom of our imagination. It is our job, no, it is our obligation, to make it present in the life of every single human being alive, especially our children. It is an essential part of being human. Art is about surviving in a world without a safety net, living in a world where we have to rely on our imaginations to address unbelievable problems. Art is about the power to make meaning, even when our world is full of meaninglessness. It is through the power of our imagination to solve problems that we can clean the air, purify the water, protect the environment and preserve the food supply. This is where art is an essential element of our ecology. Art is the voice of deep ecology - art is the metaphor of the human environment. We must teach this to our children. We must act on this hope and teach them to act on it. We must believe in hope again and we can't do this without metaphor. Metaphor is the final freedom.

The Power of Naming

I have seen people become involved in "telling their story." I have witnessed them singing songs and telling the story of their lives, even though the story was about someone else's life. No rules, no evaluations, no boundaries. They just did it. They didn't do it for someone else, they did it for themselves. It was raw, it was uncomfortable, and it was powerful. Mostly, it was powerful. And when it was over, their pain had been redeemed, their hopelessness had been challenged. Not because they had performed, but because they had participated. They had become involved, and in the process, they had produced something magical - they had produced meaning. They had, for those few moments, transcended their condition. As a result, they were transformed - they were no longer the same. By telling their story, they had given a name to their pain - it no longer controlled them. It no longer carried them, they carried it. This is the challenge that faces those of us in community arts development - the challenge to find new and innovative ways to reach people and to help them discover this voice within. Especially our children.

It will not be easy. We are in constant competition with the charming and alluring world of technology that makes brilliant and flashy promises of new and fascinating worlds beyond. Our job is made even more difficult since what we have to offer is not always easy, it is not always comfortable. It is not entertainment. It is not performance. It is not the easy way. It is an invitation to discover who we are and why we are this way. It is an invitation to fulfill the potential of who we can be by learning to speak the deep voice.

Robert Gard, one of the true pioneers and heroes of the community arts development movement used to tell a story that revealed who he was and who his generation was. He told of following his father one evening as he walked out into a Kansas field. By the time he got to where his father was, he was just sitting there looking out over the field, next to a kerosene lantern. As he sat there, his father talked about all of the changes going on around them, including the one that bothered him the most. He talked about the prairie grass and how it was disappearing - a metaphor for the change he was experiencing as an adult. At the end of the conversation, he said "Son, now go out and find your own prairie grass." Robert Gard's work in community arts development was his way of doing this, of finding the new prairie grass. He was driven by his "prairie visions" just as we are driven by the power of our own metaphors today. The metaphors have changed - and they will keep changing, but the need for them has remained the same.

The Final Argument

Yes, the arts add to the economy. Yes, the arts are a business, an industry. But we cannot afford to let that be our argument for why we do what we do. There is no question that the arts have an economic impact that needs to be recognized and appreciated. But that is not the value of art, that is not its worth. The value of art is that it is connected to the power of creation. And for reasons we cannot yet explain, art connects us to that same power - the power of metaphor.

The real argument for the presence of the arts being in our lives goes beyond the economy, and art as an industry, and art as social gathering. In the final analysis, all that matters is making community and the arts provide us a way to participate in community-making. Not a shallow, self-conceived community that meets our narrowed, self-serving needs. Not a fragmented, divided community consisting of only those who are "like" us or who "like" us. But the human community - in all of its glorified and magnificent diversity -the good, the bad, the beautiful, the ugly, the creative, the destructive - the human community in all of its weakness and failings. The human community in all of its possibility. As people, we must be about community-making or little else we do really matters.

Today, one of the metaphors that drives us is the metaphor of rebuilding the front porch of America. And if it does motivate us to do something, then the metaphor will have a power of its own. And for those younger than we, perhaps they will have a metaphor as well- it doesn't matter what it is, as long as they have one. For if they have one, they will spend their time looking to fulfill it - and the metaphor will have power in their life. The metaphor will become their life and because of the metaphor, it will be a life of hope.

We must create community that encourages us to interact with each other, understanding that we are interdependent, that we can stand being alone as long as we have company; community that nurtures sharing, both giving and taking; community that reinforces the value of each of us as an individual and acknowledges our responsibility to those around us. This is community. It is not easy. It is not always pretty. Sometimes it is hard. But it is always worth it because this is authentic community. It is community that can be and will be sustained, protecting the future, even that of the seventh generation. It is community that is premised on the belief that who we are as human beings matters, that what we do as human beings has meaning. It is the community created by the power of our imagination to see beyond the way things are to what has always been there, waiting to be revealed. We know its name - it is contained in the marrow of our bones. Perhaps I can put it best in a poem I wrote called "The Seed of Eden."

The Seed of Eden

I have learned what is contained
in the wisdom of the ancients,
there are no gardens left
except for the one within each of us -
the seed of Eden
genetically coded with the memory
of a way of life that was
but is no more,
passed from one cell's generation to another
waiting for the chance to break through the
surface of our lives,
reclaim the wilderness,
turn lush the barren deserts of our souls.

I have learned that for every birth
there is corresponding pain,
but it is there, in the willingness to risk new life
paradise lost can be regained.
This is the genesis of our humanity -
the redeeming grace of saying, we.

I believe art is the Seed of Eden. I believe art is the deep voice that empowers us to transcend and transform. I believe art is the unconditional grace of the imagination that is a part of every human being.

If metaphor is the final freedom, then the freedom it creates is up to us. This is the art of community-making. This is the art of rebuilding the front porch of America.

Selected Bibliography

Community Arts Development

Altman, Mary & Caddy, John. *A Handbook for Rural Arts Collaborations.* Minnesota: Community Programs in the Arts, 1994.

_____. *Rural Arts Collaborations: The Experience of Artists in Minnesota Schools & Communities.* Minnesota: Community Programs in the Arts, 1994.

Arvold, Alfred. *The Little Country Theatre.* New York: The Macmillian Company, 1923.

Banfield, Edward C. *The Democratic Muse.* New York: Basic Books, Inc. Publishers, 1984.

Brownell, Baker. *Art is Action.* New York: Harper & Brothers Publishers, 1939.

_____. *The Human Community.* New York: Harper & Brothers Publishers, 1950.

Brunton, Paul. *Human Experience*: The Arts in Culture. New York: Larson Publications, 1987.

Burleigh, Louise. *The Community Theatre.* Boston: Little, Brown, and Company, 1917.

Case, V., & Case, R. *We Called It Culture: The Story of Chautauqua.* Garden City, New York: Doubleday & Company, Inc., 1948.

Cone, Adelia W. *The Value of Dramatics in the Secondary School.* Ohio Educational Monthly, LXI , 1912.

Crockett, Oscar G. *History of the Theatre.* Boston: Allyn and Bacon, Inc., 1982. Fourth Ed.

Dewey, John. *Art as Experience.* New York: Capricorn Books, 1934.

_____. *Experience & Nature.* La Salle, Illinois: Open Court, 1925.

_____, & Barnes, Albert, et. al. *Art and Education.*
        Rahway, New Jersey: Quinn & Borden Company, Inc.,
        1929.

Dreezen, Craig. *Intersections: Community Arts and Education
        Collaborations.* Amherst, Mass: Arts Extension
        Service, 1992.

Gard, Robert E., and Burley, Gertrude. *Community Theatre:
        Idea and Achievement.* New York: Duell, Sloan and
        Pearce, 1959.

_____. *Grassroots Theatre: A Search for Regional Arts in
        America.* Madison, Wisconsin: The University of
        Wisconsin, 1955.

_____, & Kolhoff, Ralph. *The Arts in the Small Community:
        A National Plan.* Washington D.C.: National Assembly
        of Local Arts Agencies, reprinted 1984.

_____. *Prairie Visions: A Personal Search for the
        Springs of Regional Art & Folklife.* Ashland,
        Wisconsin: Heartland Press, 1987.

Gibans, Nina Freelander. *The Community Arts Council
        Movement.* New York, Praeger Publishers, 1982.

Golden, Joseph. *Olympus on Main Street.* Syracuse, New York:
        Syracuse University Press, 1980.

_____. *Pollyanna in the Briar Patch: The Community Arts
        Movement.* Syracuse, New York: Syracuse University
        Press, 1987.

Gould, Joseph E. *The Chautauqua Movement.* New York: State
        University of New York, 1961.

Harris, Louis. *Americans and the Arts.* New York: American
        Council for the Arts, 1984.

Harrison, Harry P. *Culture Under Canvas.* New York: Hastings
        House Publishers, 1958.

Katz, Jonathan & North, Alice, (Eds.). *Serving the Arts in Rural
        Areas: Successful Programs and Potential New
        Strategies.* Washington, D.C.: National Assembly of
        State Arts Agencies, 1991.

Keens, William & Rhodes, Naomi. *An American Dialogue: The National Task Force on Presenting and Touring the Performing Arts*. Washington, D.C.: The Association of Performing Arts Presenters, 1989.

MacKaye, Percy. *The Civic Theatre*. New York: Mitchell Kennerley, 1912.

Mackay, D'arcy Constance. *The Little Theatre in the United States*. New York: Henry Hold and Company, 1917.

Melillo, Joseph V. *Market the Arts!*. New York: FEDAPT, 1983.

Miaoulis, George, & Lloyd, David. *Marketing the Arts in a Rural Environment: The Monadnock Arts Study*. Dayton, Ohio: Wright State University Publications, 1979.

Mitchell, Arnold. *The Professional Performing Arts: Attendance Patterns, Preferences and Motives*. Volumes I and II. Madison, Wisconsin: Association of College, University and Community Arts Administrators, Inc., 1985.

Morrison, Theodore. *Chautauqua: A Center for Education, Religion , and the Arts in America*. Chicago: The University of Chicago Press, 1974.

National Endowment for the Arts. *Toward Civilization: A Report on Arts Education*. Washington, D.C.: National Endowment for the Arts, 1988.

Orchard, Hugh A. *Fifty Years of Chautauqua*. Cedar Rapids, Iowa: The Torch Press, 1923.

Overton, Patrick (Ed.). *Spanning Cultures Through Arts Education: Asian Pacific Conference on Arts Education, Conference Proceedings*. Columbia, Missouri: The Center for Community & Cultural Studies, 1990.

_____. (Ed.). *Grassroots and Mountain Wings: The Arts in Rural and Small Communities*. Columbia, Missouri: The Center for Community & Cultural Studies, 1992.

_____. (Ed.). *Southern Illinois Cultural Planning Project: Needs Assessment Report and Recommendations.* Columbia, Missouri: The Center for Community & Cultural Studies, 1993.

Patten, Marjorie. *The Arts Workshop of Rural America: A Study of the Rural Arts Program of the Agricultural Extension Service.* New York: Columbia University Press, 1937. Reprinted, AMS Press, Inc., 1967.

Perry, Clarence. *The Work of the Little Theatres.* New York: Russell Sage Foundation, 1933.

Porter, Robert, (Ed.). *Community Arts Agencies: A Handbook and Guide.* New York: American Council for the Arts, 1978.

Rappel, William J., & Winnie, John R. *Community Theatre Handbook.* Iowa City: State University of Iowa, 1961.

Stevens, Louise K. *Conducting a Community Cultural Assessment: Work Kit.* Amherst, Massachusetts: The Arts Extension Service, 1987.

Vincent, John H. *The Chautauqua Movement.* New York: Books for Libraries Press, 1885. Reprinted, 1971.

Vinson, Elizabeth A. *For the Soul & the Pocketbook: A Resource Guide for the Arts in Rural and Small Communities.* Washington D.C.: The National Rural Center, 1981.

Von Eckhardt, Wolf. *Live the Good Life! Creating a Human Community Through the Arts.* New York: American Council for the Arts, 1982.

Wallace, Karl R. *History of Speech Education in America.* New York: Appleton-Century- Crofts, Inc., 1954.

Wilson, Garff B. *Three Hundred Years of American Drama and Theatre.* Englewood Cliffs, New Jersey: Prentice-Hall, Inc., 1973.

Yuen, Cheryl. *Community Vision: A Policy Guide to Local Arts Agency Development.* Washington, D.C.: National Assembly of Local Arts Agencies, 1990.

Young, John Wray. *The Community Theatre and How It Works.* New York: Harper & Brothers, Publishers, 1957.

_____. *Community Theatre: A Manual For Success.* New York: Samuel French, Inc., 1971.

Community-Making

Alinsky, Saul. *Rules for Radicals: A Pragmatic Primer for Realistic Radicals.* New York: Random House, 1972.

Bailey, Kenneth D. *Methods of Social Research.* New York: The Free Press, 1978.

Baker, Harold R. *Restructuring Rural Communities.* Parts 1 and 2. Saskatoon, Saskatchewan: University Extension Press, 1993.

Berry, Wendell. *What Are People For?* New York: Farrar, Straus, and Giroux, 1990.

Biddle, W., & Biddle, Loureide. *The Community Development Process: The Rediscovery of Local Initiative.* New York: Holt, Rinehart, and Winston, Inc., 1965.

Cary, Lee. (Ed.). *Community Development as a Process.* Columbia, Missouri: University of Missouri Press, 1970.

Etzioni, Amitai. *The Spirit of Community: Rights, Responsibilities, and the Communitarian Agenda.* New York: Random House, 1993.

Kramer, Ralph M. & Specht, Harry, (Eds.). *Readings in Community Organization Practice.* Englewood Cliffs, New Jersey: Prentice-Hall, 1969.

Lingeman, Richard. *Small Town America.* New York: G.P. Putnam's Sons, 1980.

Mitchell, Arnold. *The Nine American Lifestyles: Who We Are & Where We Are Going.* New York: Macmillian Publishing Co. Inc., 1983.

Peck, M. Scott. *The Different Drum: Community Making & Peace.* New York: Touchstone Books, 1987.

_____. *A World Waiting to Be Born: Civility Rediscovered*. New York: Bantam Books, 1993.

Ross, Murray G., with B. W. Lappin. *Community Organization: Theory, Principles, and Practice*. New York: Harper & Row, Publishers, 2nd Edition, 1967.

Rothman, Jack. *Planning and Organizing for Social Change*. New York: Columbia University Press, 1974.

Warren, Rachelle B. & Warren, Donald. *The Neighborhood Organizer's Handbook*. Notre Dame, Indiana: University of Notre Dame Press, 1977.

Warren, Roland. *The Community in America*. Chicago: Rand McNally & Company, 3rd Edition, 1978.

Creativity

Arieti, Silvano. *Creativity: The Magic Synthesis*. New York: Basic Books Inc. Publishers, 1976.

Boostrom, Robert. *Developing Creative & Critical Thinking*. Lincolnwood, Illinois: NTC publishing, 1992.

Gardner, Howard. *Frames of Mind: The Theory of Multiple Intelligences*. New York: Basic Books, 1983.

_____. *Creating Minds*. New York: Basic books, 1993.

Harmen, Willis, & Rheingold, Howard. *Higher Creativity: Liberating the Unconscious for Breakthrough Insights*. Los Angeles: Jeremy P. Tarcher, Inc., 1984.

Maslow, Abraham H. *The Farther Reaches of Human Nature*. New York: The Viking Press, 1971.

May, Rollo. *The Courage to Create*. New York: W. W. Norton & Company, Inc., 1975.

Neirenberg, Gerard I. *The Art Of Creative Thinking*. New York: Cornerstone Library, 1982.

Osborn, Alex F. *Applied Imagination*. New York: Charles Scribner's Sons, 1953.

Phelan, Thomas W. *All About Attention Deficit Disorder: Symptoms, Diagnosis and Treatment: Children and Adults.* Glen Ellyn, Illinois: Child Management Inc., 1996.

Raudsepp, Eugene. *How Creative Are You?.* New York: Perigee Books, 1981.

Rogers, Carl R. *On Becoming A Person.* Boston: Houghton-Mifflin Company, 1961.

Rothenberg, Albert. *The Emerging Goddess: The Creative Process in Art, Science, and Other Fields.* Chicago: The University of Chicago Press, 1979.

Taylor, I. A., & Getzels, J. W. (Eds.). *Perspectives in Creativity.* Chicago: Aldine Publishing Company, 1975.

Intercultural Communications

Bolton, Richard (ed.). *Culture Wars.* New York: The New Press, 1992.

Hirschberg, Stuart. *One World, Many Cultures* (2nd Ed.). Needham Heights, Massachusetts: Allyn & Bacon, 1995.

Inkeles, Alex & Masamichi, Sasaki. *Comparing Nations and Cultures.* Englewood Cliffs, New Jersey: Prentice-Hall, 1996.

Lusting, Myron & Koester, Jolene. *Intercultural Competence: Interpersonal Communication Across Cultures.* New York: Harper Collins, 1993.

Samovar, Larry & Porter, Richard. *Intercultural Communication* (7th Ed.). Belmont, California: Wadsworth, Inc., 1994.

_____. *Communication Between Cultures.* Belmont, California: Wadsworth, Inc., 1991.

Seelye, H. Ned. *Teaching Culture: Strategies for Intercultural Communication* (3rd Ed.). Chicago: NTC Publishing, 1993.

Stewart, John. *Bridges Not Walls: A Book about Interpersonal Communication* (6th Ed.). New York: McGraw-Hill, 1995.

Organizational Communications

Argyris, Chris. *Personality and Organization - The Conflict Between System and the Individual.* New York: Harper & Row, 1957.

Barnard, Chester. *The Function of the Executive.* Cambridge, Massachusetts: Harvard University Press, 1938.

Beckhard, Richard & Pritchard, Wendy. *Changing the Essence: The Art of Creating and Leading Fundamental Change in Organizations.* San Francisco: Jossey-Bass, Inc. Publishers, 1992.

Covey, Stephen R. *Principle-Centered Leadership.* New York: Fireside, 1992.

Deal, Terrence E. & Kennedy, Allen A. *Corporate Cultures: The Rites and Rituals of Corporate Life.* Reading, Massachusetts: Addison-Wesley Publishing Company, 1982.

French, Wendell L., Kast, Fremont E., & Rosenzweig, James E. *Understanding Human Behavior in Organizations.* New York: Harper & Row, Publishers, 1985.

Kanter, Rosabeth Moss. *The Change Masters.* New York: Simon & Schuster, Inc., 1983.

Koehler, J.W., Anatol, W.E., & Applbaum, R.L. *Organizational Communication: Behavioral Perspectives.* New York: Holt, Rinehart, and Winston, 1976.

Levinson, Harry. *Executive: The Guide to Responsive Management.* Cambridge, Massachusetts: Harvard University Press, 1968.

Naisbitt, John. *Megatrends.* New York: Warner Books, 1982.

_____, & Aburdene, Patricia. *Re-Inventing the Corporation.* New York: Warner Books, 1985.

Peters, Tom, & Austin, Nancy. *A Passion for Excellence*. New York: Random House, 1985.

Peters, Thomas J., & Waterman, Robert H. Jr. *In Search of Excellence*. New York: Harper & Row, Publishers, 1982.

Pondy, Louis R., (Ed.). *Organizational Symbolism*. Greenwich, Connecticut: JAI Press Inc., 1983.

Putnam, Linda L., & Pacanowsky, Michael E., (Eds.). *Communication and Organizations*. Beverly Hills: Sage Publications, 1983.

Schein, Edgar H. *Organizational Culture and Leadership*. San Francisco: Jossey-Bass Inc., 1985.

Senge, Peter M. *The Fifth Discipline: The Art & Practice of The Learning Organization*. New York: Doubleday, 1990.

Rifkin, Jeremy. *The End of Work: The Decline of the Global Labor Force and the Dawn of the Post-Market Era*. New York: G.P. Putnam's Sons, 1995.

Toffler, Alvin. *The Culture Consumers*. New York: St. Martin's Press, 1964.

_____. *The Adaptive Corporation*. New York: McGraw-Hill Book Company, 1985.

Nonprofit Organizations

Arnot, M., Lee, C., & Houde, M. *The Volunteer Organization Handbook*. Blacksburg, Virginia: Center for Volunteer Development, 1985.

Carver, John. *Boards That Make a Difference*. San Francisco: Jossey-Bass, Inc., 1990.

Clifton, Roger, Reinert, Richard, & Stevens, Louise. *The Road Map to Success: A Unique Development Guide for Small Arts Groups*. Boston: Massachusetts Cultural Alliance, 1988.

Connors, Tracy, (Ed.). *The Nonprofit Management Handbook: Operating Policies and Procedures*. New York: John Wiley & Sons, Ltd., 1995.

DiMaggio, Paul J. *Nonprofit Enterprise in the Arts: Studies in Mission and Constraint.* New York: Oxford University Press, 1986.

Drucker, Peter F. *Managing the Nonprofit Organization: Principles and Practices.* New York: Harper Collins Publishers, 1990.

Fisher, John. *How to Manage a Non-Profit Organization.* Toronto: Management and Fundraising Centre, Publishing Division, 1978.

Flannagan, Joan. *The Successful Volunteer Organization: Getting Started and Getting Results in Nonprofit, Charitable, Grass Roots, and Community Groups.* Chicago: Contemporary Books, 1984.

Golden, Joseph, (Ed.). *In Good Form: Paperwork that Works.* Madison, Wisconsin: Association of College, University, and Community Arts Administrators, 1985.

Houle, Cyril O. *Governing Boards.* San Francisco: Jossey-Bass, Inc., 1989.

Kotler, Phillip. *Marketing for Nonprofit Organizations.* New Jersey: Prentice-Hall, Inc., 1975.

Kurtz, Daniel L. *Board Liability: Guide for Nonprofit Directors.* New York: Moyer Bell Limited, 1988.

Kuyper, Joan. *Volunteer Program Administration: A Handbook for Museums and Other Cultural Institutions.* New York: American Council for the Arts, 1993.

MacBride, Marie. *Step By Step: Management of the Volunteer Program in Agencies.* Bergen County, New Jersey: Volunteer Bureau of Bergen County, 3rd printing, 1982.

Moore, Larry F., (Ed.). *Motivating Volunteers: How the Rewards of Unpaid Work Can Meet People's Needs.* Vancouver, B.C., Canada: Vancouver Volunteer Centre, 1985.

McDaniel, Nello & Thorn, George, (Eds.). *The Challenge of Change.* New York: FEDAPT, 1987.

_____. *Work Papers* (Vol. 1 & 2). New York: FEDAPT, 1992.

Naylor, Harriet. *Volunteers Today - Finding, Training, and Working With Them.* Dryden, New York: Dryden Associates, 1967.

O'Connell, Brian. *Effective Leadership in Voluntary Organizations.* Chicago: Association Press, 1976.

_____, (Ed.). *America's Voluntary Spirit.* New York: The Foundation Center, 1983.

Owen, Harrison. *Spirit: Transformation and Development in Organizations.* Potomac, Maryland: Abbott Publishing, 1987.

Shore, Harvey. *Arts Administration and Management: A Guide for Arts Administrators and Their Staffs.* Westport, Connecticut: Greenwood Press, Inc., 1987.

Sikes, Toni Fountain. *Resources for Personal Management.* Madison, Wisconsin: Association of College, University, and Community Arts Administrators, Inc., 1984.

Vinyard, Sue. *Megatrends & Volunteerism.* Downers Grove, Illinois: Heritage Arts Publishing, 1993.

Wilson, Marlene. *The Effective Management of Volunteer Programs.* Boulder, Colorado: Volunteer Management Associates, 1976.

_____. *Survival Skills for Managers.* Boulder, Colorado: Volunteer management Associates, 1981.

Wolf, Thomas. *Presenting Performances: A Handbook for Sponsors.* Cambridge, Massachusetts: New England Foundation for the Arts, 1977.

_____. *The Nonprofit Organization.* Englewood Cliffs, New Jersey: Prentice-Hall, Inc., 1984.

Art & Spirituality

Apostolos-Cappadona, Diane. (Ed.) *Art, Creativity, and the Sacred.* NewYork: Crossroad, 1984

Barzun, Jacques. *The Use and Abuse of Art* (A. W. Mellon
    Lectures, 1973). Princeton: Princeton University press,
    1974.

Berdyaev, Nicolas. *The Meaning of the Creative Act.* New
    York: Collier Books, 1962.

Brueggemann, Walter. *The Prophetic Imagination.*
    Philadelphia: Fortress Press, 1978.

Davies, Horton and Hugh. *Sacred Art in a Secular Century.*
    Collegeville, Minnesota: The Liturgical Press, 1978.

Bryans, Nena. *Full Circle: A Proposal to the Church for an
    Arts Ministry.* San Carlos, California: Schuyler Institute
    for Worship and the Arts, 1988.

Campbell, Joseph. *The Inner Reaches of Outer Space:
    Metaphor As Myth and As Religion.* New York: Harper &
    Row, Publishers, 1986

Devall, Bill & Sessions, George. *Deep Ecology.* Salt Lake City:
    Gibbs M. Smith, Inc., 1985.

Dillenberger, Jane and John. *Perceptions of the Spirit in
    Twentieth Century American Art.* Indianapolis Museum
    of Art, Indianapolis, Indiana, 1977.

Dillenberger, John. *A Theology of Artistic Sensibilities - the
    Visual Arts and the Church.* New York: Crossroad
    Publishing Company, 1986.

Dixon, John W., Jr. *Art and the Theological Imagination.* New
    York: Seabury Press, 1978.

Driver, Tom F. *Patterns of Grace: Human Experience as Word
    of God.* San Francisco: Harper Row, Publishers, 1977.

Eichenberg, Fritz. *Art and Faith.* Pendle Hill Pamphlet 68,
    1952.

Fowler, James W. *Stages of Faith: The Psychology of Human
    Development and the Quest for Meaning.* San Francisco,
    Harper Row, Publishers, 1981.

Fox, Matthew. *Breakthrough: Meister Eckhart's Creation Spirituality in New Translation.* Garden City, New York: Doubleday, 1977.

_____, *Original Blessing.* Santa Fe, New Mexico: Bear and Company, 1983.

_____, *A Spirituality Named Compassion.* Minneapolis, Minnesota: Winston Press, 1979.

Freire, Paulo. *Pedagogy of the Oppressed.* New York: The Seabury Press, 1970.

_____. *Pedagogy of Hope.* New York: Continuum Publishing Company, 1994.

Getlein, Frank and Dorothy. *Christianity in Modern Art.* Milwaukee: Bruce Publishing Co., 1961.

Gusdorf, Georges. *Speaking (La Parole).* Paris, France: Presses Universitaries de France, 1953. Translation, Brockelman, Paul T. Northwestern University Press, 1965.

Harned, David Baily. *Theology and the Arts.* Philadelphia: The Westminster Press, 1966.

Henri, Robert. *The Art Spirit.* Compiled by Margery Ryerson. New York: Lippincott, 1960.

Hillman, James. *The Soul's Code.* New York: Random House, 1996.

Jung, Carl G. *Man and His Symbols.* New York: Dell Publishing Company, 1964.

_____. *Modern Man in Search of a Soul.* New York: Harcourt, Brace and World, 1933.

_____. *Psyche and Symbol.* Garden City, New York: Doubleday Anchor Books, 1958.

Kandinsky, Wassily. *Concerning the Spiritual in Art.* New York: Dover Publications, Inc., 1977.

Kung, Hans. *Art and the Question of Meaning.* New York: Crossroad, 1981.

Laeuchli, Samuel. *Religion and Art in Conflict*. Philadelphia: Fortress Press, 1980.

L'Engle, Madeleine. *Walking on Water: Reflections on Faith and Art*. Wheaton, Illinois: Harold Shaw, 1980.

Maritain, Jacques & Cocteau, Jean. *Art and Faith*. New York: Philosophical Library, 1948.

May, Rollo. *The Courage to Create*. New York: W.W. Norton and Co., 1975.

McGaa, Ed. *Mother Earth Spirituality: Native American Paths to Healing Ourselves and Our World*. San Francisco: Harper Collins Publishers, 1990.

Moore, Thomas. *Care of the Soul*. New York: Harper Collins Publishers, Inc., 1992.

_____. *The Re-Enchantment of Everyday Life*. New York: Harper Collins Publishers, Inc., 1996.

Overton, Patrick. *The Leaning Tree*. St. Louis: Bethany Press, 1975.

Ouspensky, Leonid, and Valdimir Lossky. *The Meaning of Icons*. Crestwood, New York: St. Vladimir Seminary Press, 1983.

Palmer, Parker. *The Company of Strangers*. New York: Crossroad, 1981.

Purdy, William. *Seeing and Believing - Theology and Art*. Butler, Wisconsin: Clergy Book Service, 1976.

Rank, Otto. *Art and Artist*. New York: Alfred A. Knopf, Inc., 1932.

Robbins, Lois B. *Waking Up in the Age of Creativity*. Sante Fe, New Mexico: Bear and Co., 1984.

Rokeach, Milton. *Beliefs, Attitudes and Values*. San Francisco: Jossey-Bass Inc., 1968.

_____. *The Nature of Human Values*. New York: The Free Press, 1973.

_____. *Understanding Human Values*. New York: The Free Press, 1979.

Rookmaaker, H.R. *Modern Art and the Death of a Culture*. Leicester, England: Inter-Varsity Press, 1970.

Roszak, T., Gomes, M., & Kanner, A. (Eds.). *Ecopsychology: Restoring the Earth, Healing the Mind*. San Francisco: The Sierra Club, 1995.

Tillich, Paul. *The Shaking of the Foundations*. New York: Charles Scribner's Sons, 1948.

_____. *The Courage To Be*. New Haven: Yale University Press, 1952.

_____. *Theology of Culture*. New York: Oxford University Press, 1959.

_____. *Systematic Theology*, Volume III. Chicago: University of Chicago Press, 1963.